NIGHT

SEARCHING
FOR
MY
HOCKEY
HERO

* * *

JIM
HARRISON

BY
DAVID
WARD

ECW

Published by ECW Press
2120 Queen Street East, Suite 200, Toronto, Ontario, Canada M4E 1E2
416-694-3348 / info@ecwpress.com

Library and Archives Canada Cataloguing in Publication

Ward, David, 1958–, author
The lost 10 point night : searching for my hockey hero ... Jim Harrison / David Ward.

ISBN 978-1-77041-155-5
ALSO ISSUED AS: 978-1-77090-589-4 (PDF); 978-1-77090-587-0 (EPUB)

1. Harrison, Jim, 1947–. 2. Ward, David, 1958–. 3. Hockey players—Canada—Biography.
I. Title. II. Title: Lost ten point night.

GV848.5.H36W37 2014   796.962092   C2014-902570-X

Editor for the press: Michael Holmes
Cover design: David Gee
Cover image: detail from O-Pee-Chee trading card
Interior images: from the collection of Jim Harrison
Interior design: Rachel Ironstone

Printed and bound in Canada at Friesens   1   2   3   4   5

The publication of *The Lost 10 Point Night* has been generously supported by the Canada Council for the Arts, which last year invested $157 million to bring the arts to Canadians throughout the country. We acknowledge the support of the Ontario Arts Council (OAC), an agency of the Government of Ontario, which last year funded 1,793 individual artists and 1,076 organizations in 232 communities across Ontario, for a total of $52.1 million. We also acknowledge the financial support of the Government of Canada through the Canada Book Fund for our publishing activities, and the contribution of the Government of Ontario through the Ontario Book Publishing Tax Credit and the Ontario Media Development Corporation.

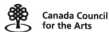

For my brother

"Let's pretend," a voice suggested, "that we're one of those Frank Capra movies."

"How do we do that?"

"You know. Here we are, up in the heavens, looking down."

"Right. And all you see on the screen is a bunch of nebulae and assorted twinklies."

"Exactly."

"With violins," another voice suggested.

"Do they like this sort of stuff?"

"Some do, some don't."

"Okay. Here we go. Look down. Look away down there. Look at the town of Falconbridge, Ontario, population, thirteen thousand."

"Thirteen thousand and one if we count him."

"There he is. Staring right back at us, coincidentally."

"Is it he with whom we are going to fuck around?"

"Well," came a voice, considering, "he's doing a pretty crackerjack job of fucking around with himself. We're going to help him."

"What's he got? Marital problems? Financial difficulties? Mental anguishes? Emotional instability? Physical abnormalities and/or diseases?"

"He's got all sorts of general problems. We're here for something specific."

"Like what, for instance?"

"You guys ever hear of a game called hockey?"

— Paul Quarrington,
Logan in Overtime

INTRODUCTION

This book is based on two premises.

One, I like sportswriter Stephen Brunt. I like him a lot — on radio, television, and in print. I like the way he sees the world in a cultural context. I like that he employs his sensibilities by simply describing circumstances and asking basic questions. Stephen practices sportswriting like it's a subtly subversive science rather than an undertaking best suited for blunt tools.

Yet I styled this book as a challenge to Stephen, because I wish he more often accessed a different group of personalities. I want to hear what he has to share about the B-list or lower — a gang who are not so guarded, because they have so little to lose.

Maybe *challenge* is not the right word. I think this book is more my *contribution* to the discussion than a confrontation or test. Because as conceited as I sound, anchoring myself alongside Brunt, I see this book as a response to *Searching for Bobby Orr* and *Gretzky's Tears*. Except that my subjects don't come from any A-list. Quite the opposite actually — I've tried to give voice to those who don't always believe they have one.

It's possible I've built the book this way because, as a first-time participant in the popular media, I can't compete. The A-list has no interest in talking to me. Or so their publicists say. But even when I do get past the uncivilized front line, the celebrated stars seldom give me anything of value compared to the jilted journeymen.

The second premise on which this book is based is that it is part biography, part memoir, and all cathartic — catharsis being the release of emotions through art. So as much as I would like to begin this book with a standard "all errors are mine," they're not. Not that I'm not accountable for my interpretations, but there are things people say that don't always support the facts. Like when an aging athlete insists he left home at a younger age than the records indicate, I don't want to deny his details. I want to share such events as the speaker remembers them, because I find it informative when subjects emphasize *their* memories.

It has been a blessing that my subject was a third-line center, that when I went in search of him he didn't immediately shut the door in my face. Because that too is what this book is about — a 50-year-old man's wish to get close to his childhood hero. I hope it's of value to you, but more than that, I'm keeping my fingers crossed that the process and the product continue to be cathartic for the author and his subject.

"What have you been up to?" a friend asks.

"Writing," I reply.

"Writing about what?"

"I went in search of my childhood hero. So I'm writing about that."

I'm aware that simply saying "childhood hero" leaves things wide open, but I'm wary of saying more because not everyone is a hockey fanatic. A lot of Canadians resent the space that hockey occupies. And many find the game too violent. Plus, there are a lot of casual fans who, when I say I'm writing a book about Jim Harrison, don't recognize his name.

"Did you say Henderson?"

"No, *Harrison*. Jim Harrison."

"What's *his* story?"

"Bruins, Leafs, Hawks, and Oilers. He wasn't a huge star but he was important to me. In the early '70s, Jim was a big, mop-topped tough guy with bushy black sideburns — the kind of guy who would just as soon run over you as score a goal. That was all pretty exciting to me as a child. I liked the stars, but I *loved* the plumbers. I was a Don Cherry kind of kid long before I knew what a Cherry was.

"Years later, Jim fell on bumpy times after injuries got the best of him, and Alan Eagleson ripped him off. Today he's trying to correct some of the injustices he's been subjected to and overcome some of the injuries he suffered."

Now, I know I lost the listener early but by saying "Eagleson," I've hit on something many Canadians remember: "Oh yeah — that crook. I'd say your Henderson buddy's not the only guy he ripped off."

"Harrison."

"What?"

"Not Henderson. Jim *Harrison*."

THE LOST
10 POINT
NIGHT

SEARCHING
FOR
MY
HOCKEY
HERO

* * *

JIM
HARRISON

*

I'm watching Leafs and Flyers, a game from February 6, 1971. I remember seeing this game as a child, live on television. I watched it from the floor of my family's modest Kitchener, Ontario, home. But today I'm viewing it on a laptop while sitting in outport Newfoundland. Thanks to the miracle of Leafs TV.

What a concept, eh? An entire television network dedicated to a terrible hockey team. Were there really folks who could have conceived of such in '71? Not that there weren't prophets who could predict the future of television and other technologies. But that fans could've imagined the next four decades would bring so little glory to their beloved blue and white, and that such pathetic play would still result in enough viewer interest to support a 24/7 TV channel.

"I'm Paul Hendrick, and welcome to this *Molson Canadian Classic 'Game in an Hour,'*" our host says, and right away I'm wondering why people in production insist on dumbing things down: why Leafs TV believes viewers require an abridged version of the original; how they assume that fans don't value the events that go on between goals, saves, and periods; and why they think we'd be intrigued with the idea of seeing only *part* of the original proceedings in one sitting — on a station that cycles the same old stuff over and over anyway.

"In the winter of 1971, the Leafs, under the guidance of general manager Jim Gregory and head coach Johnny McLellan, have themselves a formidable roster," Hendrick either informs or reminds us, "one that they hope would compete well into the following decade. However, problems would ensue a year later, as the WHA [World Hockey Association] would raid the Toronto Maple Leafs and things certainly would change, for a while." Understated? Such that Hendrick avoids articulating the arrogant role Leaf ownership played in the rival league's raid? Yes. "But in the short term, however, things were looking good . . . Just the previous week the Leafs had acquired Bernie Parent in exchange for forward Mike Walton and another goaltender in Bruce Gamble . . .

"To the gondola we go." From there we see black-and-white imagery of Dave Keon and Bobby Clarke awaiting a faceoff in the Flyers end. Leafs wear white, Flyers orange. Actually, almost everything is an attractive white, because there's no ugly advertising except for the gaudy graphics that Leafs TV employs. Graphics that, against 40-year-old footage, look so out of place they leave me embarrassed for whoever makes such aesthetic choices. It's like, who would put a bumper sticker on the *Mona Lisa*?

While play prepares to resume, we hear Bill Hewitt's nasal accent as he comments on the big trade, in which Philadelphia sent Parent and their second-round choice in the upcoming Amateur Draft — Rick Kehoe — to Toronto for Gamble, Walton, and the Leafs' first-round selection — Pierre Plante — in the same sweepstakes. The Flyers then parlayed Walton into a deal with Boston for forwards Danny Schock and Rick MacLeish. Both trades brought drama to what otherwise might have been a mundane mid-winter meeting between two mediocre clubs.

The puck is dropped and suddenly I'm 12 years old again. The Leafs of my youth are all present, exactly as I remember them: Garry Monahan and Billy MacMillan take their rightful positions alongside Keon. Jim Dorey and Bob Baun are on defence, and Jacques Plante is in goal. I find it fascinating how slender Plante is. If he played in today's game, he'd be outfitted with whatever bulk the rules would allow and then some.

Disappointed that Parent didn't start, I am pleased to see Gamble is in the Flyers' net when he flips a puck over the glass in a move that today would result in a delay-of-game penalty. I love the way neither team's coach feels compelled to change lines during the stop in play, keeping the key matchup of Keon and Clarke on the ice, in an era when shifts were much longer.

A change on the fly brings out fresh troops. Then, in a very familiar, familial way, the Leafs' Jim McKenny, behind his own net, pauses with the puck, giving teammates Paul Henderson, Norm Ullman, and Ron Ellis a chance to set up for success. Not yet three minutes old, the game has settled into an exchange of efforts to maintain puck possession when, after an uneventful shift from the Ullman line, the Harrison trio hits the ice. I readily recognize Jim Harrison not only because he is flanked by George Armstrong and Brian Spencer, but because of his clumsy skating style and Beatles hairdo.

Judging by the increased noise level in Maple Leaf Gardens, I'm not the only observer who sees there are two bangers on the ice in Harrison and Spencer. But while I wouldn't have noticed it as a child, I'm acutely aware as an adult that Armstrong, the last man to captain a Leaf team to a Stanley Cup, is playing one of the final games of his Hall of Fame career. Noticeably absent is rookie Darryl Sittler, who lost more than a third of that season to injuries.

Spencer spins. Harrison finishes a check. As Philadelphia attempts to turn up ice, a bouncing puck somehow finds its way back to the front of the Flyers' net, where Harrison stands alone. The puck skitters off his stick before he can take advantage.

"Harrison had Gamble down, but he couldn't get a shot away."

There is no way to not see the get-up-and-go this piecemeal forward line has brought to what otherwise looks like a lame game. The Flyers know they are in trouble. "Ashbee holds it against the boards." But the forechecking Harrison wants no part of his opponent's effort to postpone play. Everything about Jim's actions suggests he is saying, "Not on my watch, you won't," until he reluctantly makes his way back to the bench.

Next time the Harrison line is on the ice, it's to pick up the end of a power play. Armstrong has been replaced with Guy Trottier, a sweet little skater with a nose for the net. Trottier hits a goalpost after a nice set-up from Spencer. Then Spencer too doesn't miss by much. The Philadelphia penalty ends and, in their enthusiasm to pot a goal, all three Leaf forwards get caught up-ice, rendering it relatively easy for the Flyers to take advantage of a Plante gamble. "He scores!" Play soon resumes over the hum of public address announcer Paul Morris. "Philadelphia goal by number 21, Serge Bernier."

A homemade sign hangs in the end blues — "Against Keon's fighters, you need the Red Baron!" — an innocent attempt at inspiring the home team, representative of the heady times I grew up in.

Armstrong is back out in place of Trottier. Harrison wins the faceoff, takes a slash from Lew Morrison, and passes to Spencer. The rush is on — a dash resulting in a turnover that, during the ensuing scramble, sets up the boys for big, open-ice, high-speed hits. Harrison flattens a Frenchman. Spencer sends a message to Morrison. Even the 40-year-old Armstrong applies body along the boards.

There's 2:38 left in the first period. The camera catches a glimpse of the Harrison unit catching their breath on the bench. Then it moves to a mod sign acknowledging the fans' love for Spencer before Hewitt enunciates, "Keon, MacMillan, and Monahan facing MacLeish, Clarke, and Kelly." The latter two, as key parts of the Broad Street Bullies, will one day wreak havoc but tonight are quiet.

I watch how well Plante handles the puck. Then Hewitt crescendos to a shout: "The Leafs' Pelyk starts out, changes his mind. Over to McKenny. McKenny coming up over the blue line, closing in. Passes!" Hewitt's passion for the play fades when "MacMillan just fails to get his backhand away." It's remarkable how happy such an ordinary 40-year-old end-to-end rush resulting in nothing can make me.

The puck goes over the boards into the Leaf bench, striking Monahan hard on his helmetless head, and, in true hockey fashion, nobody notices. "Last minute to play in the period," Morris points out. Henderson, Ullman, and Ellis attempt to attack but can't quite connect before the bell sounds. Period ends, Leafs down by one. I'm in hockey heaven.

* *

Jim's posture today reminds me of what you see on his 1977 hockey card — the one where he's leaning on his stick, which sits on his thighs. Shaggy-haired, unshaven, and wearing the classic red Black Hawks sweater, he looks to be listening to a linesman.

Now he is wearing a sweatshirt and jeans. His hair, styled shorter than it was in the '70s, is still remarkably dark, hip, and thick. His body too is thick. So is mine.

I'd heard he had a hockey school in the Okanagan Valley and, after a couple of cold calls, got his number from a Jim Harrison in Penticton who occasionally receives calls "from folks looking for the hockey guy." When I told hockey's Harrison what I had in mind — that I wanted to write about him — he generously invited me to visit.

We are sitting in the living room of the ground-level Kelowna condominium he shares with his wife, Caroline. Clean, cozy, and inconspicuous, the Harrisons' home is incredibly comfortable. Except for a tasteful photo hanging in the kitchen, of Jim with his fishing buddy Bobby Orr, you'd never know you were in a hockey player's house.

He tells me he doesn't think he's better than anybody else just because he played in the NHL. "This book idea of yours sounds good," he says. "But there are lots more famous players than me you could write about. I really can't see how this is going to work for *you*. I just don't think my life has been so interesting that somebody would want to read that much about it." His voice is a contradiction — a mix of manliness generously injected with innocent joy. "Or do you need me to round up some other old players so you have a chance of writing a book that people will actually want to read?"

I stutter. "No, yeah, no — no need for other players." This was okay to say, I suppose, because I would have regrets if I said what I was thinking. That I too do not believe he is better than anybody else just because he had played pro. Not that I don't respect his hockey history, but because it is clear that all sorts of kooks and name-droppers are always trying to connect with past athletes. I want him to know I am not part of that crowd.

Plus I want him to know my reasons for searching him out are no longer about hero worship. I say *no longer* because I was once a 12-year-old Toronto Maple Leafs fan, and Jim was my favourite player. So as a boy I would have gone through the same stages of admiration for hockey stars that many other Canadian kids do. However, at 50, it is no longer like this for me. Actually, the opposite has occurred. With media scrutinizing celebrity issues like drug use and spousal abuse, I've come to conclude that athletes are unworthy of worship. My heroes today are ordinary people trying to live wholesome, hardworking lives. And I don't have to travel all the way to British Columbia to find one of those.

However, I do need to revisit my youth and a role model I adored at the time — with the belief that writing will take me into some complicated corners I desperately need to explore, with the hope that I can recapture some of the childlike joy that life has beaten out of me.

But hearing myself say I want to write a book sounds like someone declaring they have been thinking of doing a PhD. Have they any idea how much work awaits? Not that I don't recommend they pursue their goal. But to me there is something careless about commenting so casually about something requiring a huge sacrifice of time and energy. I am aware of the price that I and those closest to me must pay while I satisfy such creative wants and needs. I have seen the commitment that writing a book requires, and I have noted that expressing what amounts to a slice of somebody's life brings with it a big responsibility. And I believe that the energy spent telling someone I want to write a book is better spent writing than trying to boost my ego or fight my fears by gauging the responses of others to my dream.

Another concern I have regards writing style. I prefer a narrative approach that conveys what Jim's character means to me, and could mean to others — a style that authorities advise is badly suited for biography. Yes, I want to document the stories of an old-time player, but mostly I want to be a bridge between Jimmy David Harrison and hockey fans.

Yet my book idea is also about a middle-aged male in search of his boyhood hero and whatever waits. Because there is something to be said about the memories we collect prior to puberty. I can remember Jim centering a forward line with the dynamic rookie Darryl Sittler and the cagey veteran George Armstrong like it was yesterday. So I tell Jim about this emotional exploration that I intend to take via his story.

"Actually, my first linemates in Toronto were Army and Floyd Smith," he says. "Sittler was not there yet. Playing with George was like playing with John Bucyk in Boston. Those guys would tell me that if I just went to the front of the net they would get me the puck. Then it would suddenly happen. They're both nicknamed 'Chief' — George because he is Native but John just because he *looks* like an Indian. He's actually Ukrainian like me. George was always playing childish pranks on the plane. We wore blue blazers and grey slacks in those days, so if you fell asleep George would put an ice cube on your lap. Or if you were reading a newspaper he would start it on fire when you weren't looking."

When I tell Jim that in addition to recording his on- and off-ice adventures, I also want to write about the injustices he has seen and the sorrows of his personal and professional lives, I get a more heavy-hearted response.

"I just don't want to come across as a whiner or a complainer," he says. "Some writers have done stories on me without even interviewing me and their stories made me sound like a whiner. Look what happened to Carl Brewer. Carl was the greatest guy, and if not for him, the players would still be in the Stone Age. Carl might not have been the first guy to figure out the owners and the head of the Players' Association were in bed with each other, but he was the first guy who had the guts to say it in public. And guess what? Everyone called Carl a complainer. Even other old players said he should stop whining."

I find Jim's comments fascinating for two reasons. First, any reasonable person who actually listens to him should realize he is not a complainer; he's just not shy about stating his point of view. Second, what is the problem with being a complainer if you have valid reason? What is it about the game of hockey that players who protest are not respected, and they are expected to play hurt, and excuses are taboo? Why is it that those who do not subscribe to this formula get bullied and shunned?

When a young Wayne Gretzky had something to say, his critics called him a yapper. Little consideration was given to why he spoke out. Maybe he was less tolerant of inequities than his predecessors. Maybe he was trying to take the game and the business to a better place. Or perhaps he realized that because his extraordinary talent gave him security few shared, he had a responsibility to speak out.

Never was this more apparent than in 1983, when Gretzky described the New Jersey Devils as "a Mickey Mouse organization." It was a dressing-down that triggered an extreme public reaction, directed at the rudeness of Wayne's evaluation rather than what was an accurate assessment of a sad-sack operation.

Why did the focus become Gretzky's outburst instead of the fact that Devils fans had suffered through nine consecutive outrageously bad years? Why did people not rejoice in Wayne's effort to point out the obvious in hope of change for the better? And why are ownership and management not burdened by this same judgment? When an owner expresses himself in an outspoken manner, he is considered a passionate investor who wants only the best for his club. When a general manager fights for changes he deems necessary, the majority see him as a thinker. Yet a young Sidney Crosby was branded a yapper 25 years after Gretzky. Why is it that when a player expresses himself, hockey labels him as unprofessional and focuses negatively on his efforts to influence change?

Jim recalls a conversation he had with former Calgary Flame Jim Peplinski when he attempted to express his concerns about how corruptly their Players' Association had handled some things in the past. "Peplinski said I should let it go," Jim tells me. "It was a privilege to play the game — to be part of the NHL *family*, he called it. He said I should focus on that."

Comments like these cause Jim to lie awake at night and wonder what he is doing wrong.

"It's not that I'm not grateful for everything hockey has given me," he says. "I am. I loved the game. Still do. The people I met and the places I went and the things I did and the fun we had . . . I am glad to tell you all my stories. I'm just afraid I might come across as a whiner or a complainer when I talk about my injuries, finances, and some of the things some of the guys who ran hockey have done to me and others."

Hearing Jim's hurt, I am reminded how those who once ran the hockey business took advantage of the difference in attitude and love of the game between those who played and those who financed and managed the events; I'm reminded of how businessmen and bureaucrats have, for a hundred years, indirectly encouraged the idea that players who complain are not to be respected, because so-called complainers might interfere with the businessman's pursuit of power and money.

Because I grew up watching just such a model when NHL Players' Association head and convicted felon Alan Eagleson kept his constituency at arm's length by making them believe they had nothing of value to say. And by convincing them they did not have the tools to express themselves. The whole time he was stealing from them and helping NHL owners do the same.

* * *

"Yes I do, Jim. I know who Al MacInnis is. He's a Cape Breton boy
who played his junior hockey in my hometown." I want to tell Jim
of the other Hall of Fame defencemen I watched learn their craft
in Kitchener — Larry Robinson, Paul Coffey, and Scott Stevens.
I also want him to know that I know that while Robinson and
Coffey come from Winchester and Weston, Stevens was actually
born in Kitchener. But I refrain from trying to impress.

Jim: "I saw MacInnis at a charity banquet. I told him how bad
my back hurts. And how I believe our Players' Association owes me,
because it's been proven in court that they are responsible for some
of my injuries and keeping me from collecting money I'm owed.
I told him this is all in Russ Conway's book *Game Misconduct* —
how my situation played a role in Eagleson's conviction. MacInnis

was surprised to hear my lawsuit hadn't been settled.

"Lots of guys act surprised when I tell them that my [formal] claim [for compensation] hasn't been settled. I'm not sure if MacInnis just said that, but I've seen it before — how guys who played after I did can't believe my situation hasn't been sorted out.

"But the older guys are not surprised. They say the players who made the big bucks don't want to share a cent with us. That they are just waiting for us to die so we'll leave them all alone.

"I heard lots of guys say that about Eric Lindros when he worked with the Players' Association — that he didn't give a shit about the old players." Then, with an angry look, Jim asks, "Lindros comes from over your way, doesn't he?"

"W-w-well, he's from London. But that's an hour's drive from Kitchener."

"Same thing — he's from the East." Only now he's got a great big grin.

I'm obviously not the only fan who finds it fun to play "hockey geography" — knowing the birthplace of those who played the game. I figured out early that Brian Spencer was from Fort St. James, British Columbia; Ron Ellis from Lindsay, Ontario; and Alex Faulkner, the first Newfoundlander to play in the NHL, was born in Bishop's Falls. Heck, *Hockey Night in Canada* has made a fortune from loyalty to location ("Good Kingston boys!") and the accompanying alienation of others.

Maybe it was my small-town roots, but for some reason I didn't care enough to remember that Mike Pelyk, for example, was born in Toronto. And I'm not sure I want to believe the bigotry behind me not knowing the Quebec birthplace of a great goalie like Jacques Plante. Or why it took me until late in life to care that Sweden's Borje Salming came from a community called Kiruna. Perhaps I can simply assume it is not uncommon for a young boy to gravitate toward that which he finds familiar, and not all the messages I learned as a child were admirable.

Aware that Jim was born in northeast Alberta in 1947, I ask him what Bonnyville was like in the '50s. "I'm not from Bonnyville," he barks. "I'm from Glendon. But the nearest hospital was in Bonnyville, so that's where I was born. Every hockey card since says I'm from Bonnyville and that pisses Glendon people off."

"That's like Sittler," I say. "The records declare he's from Kitchener, but everyone around there knows he's from St. Jacobs, a Mennonite village north of Waterloo."

Jim's not done talking about *his* hometown: "Garry Howatt of the Islanders and the Canucks' Stan Smyl are from the Glendon area too."

After noting that all three of these Glendon men fought well outside their natural weight class, I ponder the probability that three boys from such a sparsely populated region could go on to lengthy NHL careers. Then I ask again, "So what was *Glendon* like in the '50s?"

"Rough. We were poor."

We're sitting in a comfortable but cluttered Kelowna sports bar. It's covered with autographed glossies. I'm checking out our waitress but Jim has eyes only for his large plate of perogies. He's also very excited to be talking about family: "There was me, my mom and dad, my two brothers, and my mother's six brothers — all under the same roof. My dad, Floyd, had a lumberyard that burned to the ground with no insurance, so we moved to Kamloops, where he worked at what he could. He died of heart problems when I was 18. I don't remember him very well. But when my mom wrapped her arms around me, you'd think a bear was hugging you. I remember her saying she was beaten as a child. You don't forget when you hear something like that, do you?

"They were busy people," he continues. "Dad worked long hours for low wages and Hurricane Annie fed the hungry. She had 10 of us to take care of and I remember other Ukrainians travelling by boxcar, folks on the move who my mom would feed if she could.

"She and my dad are both buried in Glendon. When I look back, it surprises me my mother let me go play junior hockey in Saskatchewan when I was only 15. 'Why'd you let me go?' I asked her years later. 'Because I knew you'd go anyway,' she said.

"Hockey with my brothers Ron and Ray was a big part of my life. I pretended I was Andy Bathgate like I guess you pretended you were me," Jim says, a little self-consciously. "But all I knew about Andy Bathgate was what I heard on the radio. We didn't have a television.

"It's funny to think about it now — how you pick your heroes. Because Andy Bathgate was known for his skating, which was never the strongest part of my game. And Andy was not known for his fighting, yet I don't remember a time when I didn't fight. I never needed a reason. Years later I realized this wasn't the way it was for everybody. I'd see the fear in some of the Swedes in the '70s, when they figured out that there were guys like me who could kill them just because they came from somewhere else.

"See, I learned to hate the French and guys from Ontario. We didn't like the French, just because they were French. And the Ontario guys, because they got everything easy. To be honest, I haven't really changed my mind about these things.

"I remember European players who booked advance plane tickets home on dates when their team could have still been in the playoffs. They had decided they were out [of the running for the Stanley Cup] already, that their team would be eliminated when that day to fly home arrived. While they know now not to get caught doing stuff like that, I believe there are still European players who think that way — guys who just want to go home when the going gets tough and the big paycheques stop.

"Not that I don't know some great guys from the east or that I don't respect some French players. Just that it's tough for me to change the way I've always been."

Jim is watching international hockey. I am browsing through boxes of newspaper clippings that Jim's mother collected, honouring his on-ice achievements. Caroline has just come from the kitchen. As she hands me a cup of green tea to help me nurse a cold I'm carrying, I ask her what *she* thinks of Glendon. A woman of more careful tendencies than her blustery husband, Caroline — who was born in Edmonton but raised in Quesnel, British Columbia — informs me, "Glendon is nice. But to me, Glendon is no longer rough like Jim remembers it. People appear to have made some money from farming and oil exploration. For example, in a recent visit we saw what once had been Jim's grandfather's house but today's an old outbuilding."

While I am pleased with her reply, Caroline must have continued to consider my question, because a short time later, as I peruse an old Leaf program, she reports back to me: "One thing I do want to say, David, is that Jim *loves* his hometown. I wish you could see how worry-free and happy he gets when he goes home to Glendon."

* * * *

A lot of Canadian men born in the decade after World War II have
a similar struggle — a struggle rooted in trying to fit into two
different worlds.

There is the ultra-masculine one they were born into — a
world soldiers returned to with strong ideas, justifiably shaped,
about how their sons should be raised. And the world of today,
full of change and choices far greater than was present when these
post-war boys were born.

It is especially challenging for those who were further shaped
during that post-war period by the world of organized sports — a
highly competitive, cutthroat world where men have an enormous
interest in keeping things as they've always been; a world that to
this day is seen as less than progressive.

"I remember crying and wanting to be home in Kamloops," Jim recalls about his introduction to junior hockey in 1964. "I'd broken my wrist and I think management was afraid that if I went home I wouldn't come back. A lot of guys went home. But others stuck with it. I think there's some kind of stick-to-it toughness we produce in small Canadian towns. That's why we get so many good hockey players from the prairies.

"So the club gave me things to do that kept me with the team. I cleaned the rink, shaved the ice, and drove the bus to out-of-town games. They let me drive because I drove a truck in the summer. It was fun being part of that club.

"Playing junior in a small town was a good thing for a youngster. In a big city you can get lost. In a small town everyone knows who you are and keeps an eye on you.

"Like the night I scored three goals in 24 seconds in the last minute of play [to clinch a come-from-behind win] over Regina. That might not have been such a big deal if I'd played in Edmonton, but in Estevan they've never forgotten it. There are still people who tell me they went to that game," Jim says earnestly. Then he laughs as if there's more to the story. "But they were in the parking lot when I scored those goals. They'd already left the arena thinking we were going to lose."

I ask about off-ice leadership, and Jim is happy to oblige. "My coach in Estevan was Scotty Munro. He's dead now, which is too bad because you'd have loved to meet him. He taught me not only how to play hockey but also how to live. What can I say? I used to get into trouble in town. We didn't go to dances to dance, eh? But Scotty explained things to me about life. He helped me a lot. He taught me how to shake hands. I didn't know what a shirt and tie were before Scotty got hold of me.

"It was Scotty who brought me to Saskatchewan," Jim recalls. "He got word from one of his players that I could play a little. This guy had seen me in some meaningless game when I fought the

Shmyr brothers. I was just a kid and it was only a summer game. I didn't know any better. But Scotty got word and invited me to Estevan. He got me to sign a C-form, meaning I would belong to Boston for $250. Then they paid me 15 bucks a month. That was enough for me to hang out at the pool hall.

"And Ernie McLean, who coached those teams with Scotty, helped me a lot. Ernie was a good influence. He used to spend as much time trying to build the person as he did the player. Those guys are legends in western Canada. And playing junior for them kept me out of jail."

Ernie McLean coached junior hockey for 25 years, winning coaching awards, league championships, and Memorial Cups. My first memory of him is from the spring of '77. I was in high school, putting in time in "Tech Hall"; *tech* in that era meant machinery for shaping steel. Mostly, I just stood around the hallway talking hockey and passing judgment on anyone and everyone who walked by, while Prism pounded out "Spaceship Superstar" from the cafeteria jukebox.

One of my friends was telling me about a powerhouse hockey club playing for the Memorial Cup — the New Westminster Bruins. "They've got a big guy on defence, Barry Beck, and a super-coach named Ernie McLean. You've got to watch that team," my buddy told me in no uncertain terms. "They're going to win the Memorial Cup this year."

Thirty years later, I phone the fabled McLean. "I can't talk right now," he tells me. "I'm driving. But if you call me tomorrow morning I'll be happy to talk to you about Jimmy. He had an interesting career."

Extremely active, despite his advanced age, Ernie proves difficult to further track down. Partly due to his job in the mining industry, which includes regular treks into the British Columbia and Yukon wilderness to prospect for gold, and partly because Ernie gives a lot of time to charities. It takes more than a dozen phone calls to four different numbers at various locations, where Ernie isn't free to talk, before we finally link up at his New Westminster home.

"Sorry about that, buddy," he says of our difficulty in connecting, before busting ajar a door to his extensive network of friends. "What about Ross Lonsberry? He's from Watson [Saskatchewan], but he's in Los Angeles now. You've got to talk to Roscoe about Jimmy-boy, no? Ross went with Jim to the Edmonton Oil Kings when they played Oshawa for the Memorial Cup. Bobby Orr was on that Oshawa team. At the time, Orr was the best prospect in eastern Canada, and many thought Jim was the best in the West.

"And Dale Hoganson," Ernie calls out. "You've got to talk to Dale. He played junior with Jim, and he played in Los Angeles like Ross did and in the WHA like Jim did. Dale went back to North Battleford to live when he was done playing. I bet you'll find him in the Saskatchewan phonebook.

"And you've got to talk to Grant Erickson — smart guy, that Grant. He played with Jim too. He lives on Vancouver Island now. He was a coach in Victoria with the Cougars when Grant Fuhr and the Courtnall brothers played there.

"What about Chappy — John Chapman? What? You haven't talked to John? He played with Jim in Estevan. Just a minute, I'll ask my wife to get me Chappy's number. John was a great junior coach and now he's a pro scout with Philadelphia. Hang on a minute. Fran, pass me John's number, will you? It's in my jacket pocket there. Thanks. Got your pen ready, David?

"Those are the four. Yeah, those are the four guys you've got to talk to if you want to know anything about Jim's time in junior."

I tell Ernie that Jim has described him as the best storyteller in the world and I wonder if he has a tale he wants to tell me about himself.

"April 19, 1971, I was in a plane crash — we iced up," he says. "That crash cost me the sight in my left eye. And while I'm lying there in the bush, I said to myself, 'If I ever get out of here alive, no more construction work for me.' So next time I talk to Scotty I tell him, 'I'm okay, but find a place to move the hockey club.' And we ended up moving it to New Westminster. That's what I'm thinking about while I lay there almost dead — hockey."

"What was coaching Jim like, Ernie?"

"Jim had a difficult time at the start. He was an aggressive kid — hard to handle. I remember once I went on a road trip to San Diego to see the Gulls play. When I got home, Jim wasn't doing well. He wasn't playing much. But when I got back behind the bench, he responded immediately to me. We worked well together.

"Then one summer he ballooned up. His weight went up to 225 pounds when he should have been 185. He said, 'You guys want me to get in shape, don't you?' I told him, 'Don't get in shape for us. Get in shape for yourself. If you don't get in shape, no one will want you.'

"Another time we were playing in Manitoba, against Flin Flon. Bobby Clarke and Reggie Leach played for that club. I asked Jim not to fight. No matter what, I told him, it was important he stayed out of the penalty box. I wanted to win and to do that we needed him on the ice. Well, the Bombers carved him up pretty good, and they hit him every chance they got. But he wouldn't retaliate because I'd asked him not to. He told me later, 'I hope you *never* ask me to do that again.' That's how hard it was for him. But that's the type of player he was, putting the team first like that."

"Why'd you never coach in the NHL, Ernie? You had lots of success."

"The NHL promised us development money in exchange for the players they drafted from us. Then Los Angeles drafted one of our guys and I told their general manager George Maguire they owed us $20,000 for him, and he said the WHA wasn't paying it, so they weren't going to either.

"So I sued the entire NHL. League president Clarence Campbell called me and he was upset. I told him junior hockey needed that development money. But those NHL guys don't like being told what to do. So they blackball you when you try, even if you are only after what they owe you." Ernie laughs a confident laugh. "Just ask Jimmy. He knows exactly what I'm talking about. Like, do you think you could get Bob Pulford to say something for your book about Jim?"

* * * * *

John Chapman's an enigma. He's got a macho voice and a heroic, manly reputation — he once dove into a cold lake to rescue a drowning woman and her baby. Yet he effortlessly accesses and shares what's going on in his heart, as only a man who's comfortable with his emotions could do.

"My wife, Jan, like Jimmy's late wife, Liz, died of breast cancer. Jim and I have that in common," John tells me from his home in Lethbridge, Alberta. John is the first of the four I find — "the four" being the men who were boys in Estevan, the ones Ernie McLean said I needed to talk to if I hoped to understand what life was like for a teenage Jim Harrison.

"Also, like Liz, Jan was a tiny woman," John continues. "But Bobby Clarke told me, when we learned Jan had nine months to live, 'You'll be surprised how tough the tiny ones are, John.' And Clarkie was right — Jan lasted 20 months.

"One thing I did to cope, I kept a daily journal documenting Jan's battle with the disease. There's a publisher looking at it, but I didn't write it to sell it. I'm just hoping it will be of help to someone else one day."

Then, with a quick deke, John changes topics — not to get away from a sensitive subject, but to take a different kind of trip down memory lane. "Shit, Jim and I were barely 16 when we signed our C-forms," he says. "He was a hard-nosed kid with his hair slicked back into a ducktail, and I was the crew-cut, I suppose.

"After a game, we'd be given a sandwich in a box and, if we were lucky, an extra-large chocolate milk. Then we'd walk for miles in 30-below weather, carrying our gear the whole way. We'd hang our equipment to dry and then walk all the way back to our boarding house. It would be two o'clock in the morning before we were done. Yet we loved it."

"When you started coaching junior hockey," I point out, "you weren't a lot older than your players, John. Did you see this love of the game in them as well? Or did you see something different?"

"You know, I've coached some of the game's big stars — Lanny McDonald, Bob Nystrom, John Davidson, the Sutters — and I'll tell you, when you sit around having a couple of beers with those boys, they don't talk about their Stanley Cups or their pro careers. You know what they talk about? They talk about two things. One, their days in junior hockey — because it is such an influential time in a young boy's life. So they talk about their teammates from that era, and their billets. They remember the people who helped them along the way.

"And second, they talk about their families. I'll tell you, Jimmy and I go back many years. We went our separate ways at 20, but you never lose that connection. So if we sat down to talk today, we'd talk about playing junior hockey together. And we'd talk about . . ." John pauses to compose himself, his voice cracking. "We'd talk about our wives."

It was just like Ernie said it would be: Dale Hoganson was in the North Battleford phonebook. But Dale had something urgent to ask when I told him his former coach had recommended I talk to him. He wanted to know if Ernie had anything to say about his near-death experience.

Now, if someone had asked me that question a couple of weeks earlier, I'd have assumed they meant the time Ernie's plane went down in northern Saskatchewan. But Ernie had recently been back in the news. He'd gone missing again, this time in the B.C. bush. Not a highly recommended practice for anyone, but especially a man of Ernie's age.

I tell Dale I spoke with Ernie *before* he went missing, but I talked with John Chapman *since* he was found, and John saw an interview with Ernie's wife, Fran. John told me that after they found Ernie alive, they asked Fran what she was going to do when she next saw him. She said, "First I'm going to hug him, and then I'm going to slap him."

Dale snorts a short chortle before adding, "I don't doubt old Ernie has made it hard on Fran over the years."

Relaxing at his home, where it is barely October but has snowed four inches on this day, Dale describes his current life, speaking in a natural rural vernacular. "We've got some land, some quarter horses, and we do a little roping. I got hitched late in life, married a local girl, she's a nurse. My daughter is in Red Deer studying to be a nurse too, and she's a hockey player. I manage my best friend's Chrysler store. We're cow people, eh?

"Yep, North Battleford is a good place to get away from the plastic part of the world. Sometimes I look at those alumni guys playing 60 old-timer games a year in Ontario and think, 'Maybe I should live there. Maybe I could make some good money.' Then I think again — 60 games a year for 30 years? How do you listen to the same old stories over and over for 30 years in a plastic part of the world?"

"Do you miss the game, Dale?"

"Well, I'll tell you — I'd been playing for Quebec but I'd just retired, and my old team was playing in Edmonton, so I went up to see the boys. I went in the dressing room and it's great, seeing the old guys. Then, after the game, we go out together and we're having a few laughs. We're talking about all kinds of things when — I'd say 20 minutes, a half-hour later — they start talking about their last game and their next game. Of course, I've got nothing to say about that so I start looking around, wondering what I'm doing there.

"That's the edge they play on. They do that every day — all hockey, all the time. I'm sure I did the same thing. It's like, they're great guys, and then suddenly it's gone. In the end, some guys can't handle that, it's so hard on them. But do *I* miss playing? Nope."

I have to ask, "Is this an okay time to talk, Dale?" Because I can hear an exciting life in the background, full of shrieks and laughter.

"Yeah, this is a great time. My wife and her brother are cleaning some geese the neighbour shot, and I'm not going to be cleaning no critters tonight. I don't mind shooting them out of the air, but I want no frigging part in what they're doing. I'd rather talk about Jim Harrison. Because when I think about my hockey career, one of the first guys I think of is Jim. We roomed together in junior. I was two years younger than he was and I held him in reverence. You know, it's not often your team's top center is your toughest guy too. And while I played with some great players on a Cup-winning team in Montreal, I've got to tell you — Jim was one of the top leaders I ever played with."

Next stop: Grant Erickson. But I was bewildered. I had no recollection of Jim's former teammate. Not that I expect to know every hockey name Ernie pulls out of Jim's past, but because Grant's career statistics — 10 years of playing pro from Rhode Island to Iowa, including a stint with the Bruins and the Minnesota North Stars, and four solid years in the WHA — aren't something I would've thought I'd have missed in my hockey-crazed youth. So I ask Jim for a little background on his buddy.

"Grant finished school in a time when most of us didn't," he says. "Plus he skipped grades along the way. Smart guy, that Grant."

Now, let's face it, old-time hockey players are not often described as "smart," although much of this judgment is a form of levelling done by insecure non-athletes. It's been my experience that, while many may not be book smart, lots of old-timers demonstrate a high level of street smarts. But any way you look at it, I was intrigued by Jim's description of Grant "Fuzzy" Erickson — the nickname resulting from Grant's inability to grow adequate facial hair.

"Wherever he played, Grant was the most popular player. He's retired now but he was in the antique business," Jim tells me. His tone reveals a lofty level of affection for his subject. "He was a trooper of a hockey player. I'm telling you, if you've ever seen a bronco rider from the rodeo — that was Grant. He was so brave. I remember we were playing Thunder Bay in the Memorial Cup, and in those days you sat in the same penalty box as the other team, so I whispered to Grant, who was just a skinny little kid at the time, 'When I drop my gloves, duck, because I'm going over top of you to punch the other guy sitting in the box beside us.' Fuzzy looked at me like I was crazy, but he wanted no part of ducking. He was coming with me.

"Another time, when I was with Edmonton and Grant in Cleveland, he took the puck off me. So I elbowed him, busted his nose up pretty good. Boy, he was pissed off. See, I'm the kind of guy who can be your buddy off the ice, but on the ice I'm different. I used to fight with Pat Quinn all the time even though we were buddies and our wives were buddies. Grant got over it, but he was ticked that night. He believes a friend shouldn't do something like that. We were supposed to go for a bite after the game but he walked right past me."

Grant speaks with me from his home, 45 kilometres north of Victoria, B.C. It's January and I'm in Fenelon Falls, Ontario, bracing for high winds and a temperature of negative 23 degrees Celsius. But because Grant is too polite to brag about the weather at his home — the temperature at Cobble Hill reached three degrees before breakfast — he chose instead to point out that he "experienced some cold days growing up in Pierceland, Saskatchewan."

After we briefly discuss a book we've both read, Grant explains how he still follows hockey but believes it would be more fun if it wasn't so "coach-controlled and robotic." Then he conveys his and Jim's common hockey history. "I played with him in four different leagues," Grant says. "We played junior together in Estevan and minor-pro in Oklahoma City. Then we both went up to Boston, and later we met up in Cleveland in the WHA."

Like Jim, Grant sounds happy about their 45-year friendship. But, awkward with any suggestion that he is "smart," Grant executes a perfect deflection, sharing an opinion on Jim instead. "Heck of a hockey player, even through his injuries. As long ago as junior, I would occasionally have to tie his skates for him, but he wouldn't say a word about how much he was hurting. That's the kind of perseverance he demonstrated his entire career. He was a great player when he was hurting, and something really special when he was healthy. Imagine what he could have done if he'd been healthy his whole career.

"Even decent medical care might have altered Jim's future. In those days, it was different. When someone talks about a 'trainer' today, I picture the equipment manager in our era trying to do both those jobs and more. They didn't have the knowledge they do now. None of us did.

"Doctors didn't know then what they do now, either." Grant is speaking from the perspective of having been on the receiving end of five knee operations, two elbow surgeries, the setting and resetting of several broken bones, and many other ailments. "And when you had a knee operation in those days, they didn't just go in with a scope — they cut you wide open. Today, some athletes are playing golf two weeks after they're operated on. In our day, you'd have to wear a big plaster cast.

"Off-ice exercise and diet were different also. We didn't take care of ourselves the way they do now. I went back to Cleveland for a reunion and the team owner gave us a tour of their new arena. I noticed a fridge full of beer in the dressing room. He said the players seldom touched the beer in that fridge. Times are different. There's so much more money involved in the game, and players are so conscious of their careers, they might take one or two beer now and then. Not like in the old days. I mean, when Jim and I played, we wouldn't have just drunk all the beer — we'd have taken the whole fridge."

I catch up with Ross Lonsberry in Los Angeles. With a style of communication that exudes both confidence and humility — two Stanley Cups and two bouts with cancer can balance a man — Ross, a successful insurance professional, gives me a nice bit of time out of his day.

"How's Jimmy doing?" Ross asks. "Would it be presumptuous of me to ask for his phone number?" He genuinely wants to know how his old buddy is getting along. "Jim and I might not have been in contact much lately, but we were once quite close," Ross says with a hint of sadness.

Then he opens up. How junior coaches Munroe and McLean had a rule that their stars weren't allowed to fight in the playoffs and how such orders would haunt these players throughout their careers. "I remember Bobby Clarke, when I played with him on those Philadelphia teams, saying something about how Harrison, in junior, would turtle whenever Estevan would meet Flin Flon in the playoffs. So I would defend Jim by telling Clarkie that Jim was just following coaches' orders.

"I mean, shit, those playoff series against Clarke's Bombers were holy wars, and there were years when I was the top player, so Scotty would tell *me* not to fight. I actually don't agree with that rule. It sets your best players up for an undeserved reputation that travels with them their entire lives. I remember once, in Fort William, I just couldn't take it anymore so I dropped my gloves. But Scotty didn't like me doing that so he sent Jim over the boards to settle things, and I remember Jim cartwheeling right over me to get at this guy *I* wanted to fight.

"Where's Fuzzy living these days? And where did you find Chappy? That's good you spoke with Dale. I remember everybody in Estevan looking at each other the first time Jim appeared on the scene. We all wondered who this thug was — he was just so rough-edged. He was the typical guy from the wrong side of the tracks. And he got hurt a short time after showing up. So here is this guy with a big chip on his shoulder, doing the team's laundry and travelling with the club, but not playing. We had no idea how good he was, much less how good he'd become. But we were pretty sure that when he got healthy, he'd be up for playing it tough."

* * * * * *

I've searched for answers to the question, *why*, at age 11, did I choose hockey as my obsession? Outside of the sport's obvious attractions — its speed and physicality — I've come to conclude it was simply circumstances that led to my connection with the game. There was an infrastructure in place to support any predisposed passion I possessed. Television had arrived, both in our culture and my home, and an hour down the road there was an NHL team that competing media outlets were eager to report on.

A more useful inquiry might be, *what* contributed to my attachment to the game? I've decided it was mostly that there was a professionally proportioned rink in my town, and that rink was a home for junior hockey. Because as wonderful as TV hockey was, it had little of the power the live event did to make me feel like an integral part of the entire affair. No, nothing came close to fulfilling my deep-seated need to dream day in and day out about what it might be like to be part of a well-run, high-level team. Ranger hockey at the Kitchener Memorial Auditorium was my pipeline to such possibility.

Often I'd take public transit there, and other times my mother would drive me in our '61 Mercury Comet. Either way, I couldn't get inside that rink fast enough. After a brief stop at the communal urinal, I would race through the smoke-filled concessions concourse, past the angry old men acting as ushers, into the awaiting arena. No matter how much I had anticipated such splendid sensations — luminous lights, an ammonia aroma, and the echo of vulcanized rubber striking wood — that arena never failed to appear more beautiful than I had remembered it.

"The Aud" was a wonderful place for me to escape the pressures of puberty and a home life ruled by an angry alcoholic and an obstinate egomaniac. Today, as an adult wishing to relive the cherished parts of that childhood, I take every opportunity to visit an assortment of junior hockey rinks across Canada.

Yet whenever I do, there is always one nagging, sad thought that sits in the seat beside me. My belief that if circumstances had been different — if I'd lived closer to Maple Leaf Gardens, for example — I might have been a victim of the same sexual abuse that some other young boys who followed the game in that era were casualties of, simply because they had heroes and dreams that rendered them vulnerable to predatory, pedophiliac arena employees.

"As you know, I have fond memories of playing junior hockey," Jim tells me. "It's the last time I played the game for free — the last time I played purely for fun. But I think it's important that people know that not everything about my junior experience was perfect. It was in junior that I saw my first sign that there were some pedophiles involved in the game. Not that we knew what a pedophile was, but there were always whispers about certain guys

— people would share words about what they thought was going on. No doubt some of the guys in charge knew.

"I'm not saying I would have known how to handle things if I'd been in management's or ownership's shoes. But some guys who were in charge back then, today pretend they didn't know that teenage boys were being sexually assaulted — on *their* watch — and that makes them liars about a hideous crime.

"So when you see the personal problems some former players have, and then you remember they played for one of those pedophiles — or you remember hearing certain guys' names being whispered along with the name of one of those bastards who abused young boys — that's a very sad part of junior hockey history."

"Who do you mean by 'bastards,' Jim?"

"I mean guys like Graham James, who coached in Moose Jaw, and Brian Shaw in Edmonton. They're the pedophiles who come to mind for most people who followed hockey in western Canada. But in Estevan we had our own — a wealthy priest named Father Finnan. To this day I'm not clear on what his involvement was with the club. We'd be at a team meal and he would ask a young, shy, weak player to pay the bill and he would tell the player to keep the change. Obviously, a guy like Father Finnan had a lot of power over us kids. He tried something on me once. He put his hand on my leg while we sat at some dining room table. I pulled away, but when you're young, you're afraid.

"Another time, there was this butcher who hung around with Father Finnan. So the rumours were always there about him. But I didn't know about them until after he invited me to stay at his house. It was after the season ended and we'd had a couple of beers when he said, 'Oh, I'll give you a ride home and you can stay with me.' I thought he was just offering me a place to crash.

"So I'm lying there in bed, and you've got to remember, I didn't know anything about pedophiles. My parents never talked to me about anything like that. Nobody did. So I'm only 15 years old, and this guy crawls into bed beside me and starts rubbing his hand against my leg. Suddenly I'm thinking, 'What do I do? I'm with an adult, he's one of the sponsors of our team, and he's always around the hockey club.' It crosses your mind in that situation that if you do what you want to do — if you tell him to go to hell — that you may never play organized hockey again. I just jumped up and said, 'I want to go home — take me home.' So he took me home. But I was pretty shook up. Then I just tried to forget about it. But you never really forget about those kinds of things, do you?

"Like later, when I was playing pro in Edmonton, Shaw was there coaching. One day, he put his hand on my leg while I lay on the training table. I pulled away that time too. Then the next day at practice, he was standing on the bench yelling at me to skate harder. I took my stick and threw it, helicopter-like, into the stands and it crashed into the seats just over his head.

"That shut him up and he left me alone after that. But it's no wonder I didn't last in Edmonton. Threatening to take a coach's head off is not a good career move. Though I actually had some of my younger teammates thank me later for sending him a message to keep away. But you don't threaten a guy like that just because he's yelling at you to skate harder. I'm pretty sure I was pissed off at him for being a pedophile.

"Another time, in an Edmonton newspaper story, I said something about pedophiles in hockey, and a guy who'd been abused called me up and thanked me for going public [with the problem]. He said it helped him that I did, which was brave of him to say. Because nobody likes to admit they were abused.

"This is something I really feel strongly about. You know, if it wasn't for people that helped me when I was a kid, where would I be? If someone had taken advantage of me, I could have easily been in bad shape today. If I had gone with Father Finnan when he tried to tempt me with money . . . Fifty-dollar bills are what he used to entice guys with. Fifty bucks was a lot of money in the '60s, especially to a kid.

"And Father Finnan didn't just go after hockey players. He always had other kids around him — high school kids and kids from the choir. So how many lives did Father Finnan ruin? Not that I know for sure what went on, but it was wrong. It was wrong for him to be so close to so many young boys the way he was, flashing $50 bills."

Jim is troubled by this topic. Agitated actually. "Perhaps more than anything else, I wish people knew a little more about this whole pedophile thing. Sports are a big influence on a child's life, and it's a shame when somebody takes advantage of that.

"And I was one of the more fortunate ones, going to Estevan like I did. It might not have been perfect there, but I lucked out going to Estevan and not some Mickey Mouse club where there were lots of guys hanging around for all the wrong reasons. That would have been terrible — to have ended up somewhere where all they wanted to do was use and abuse me.

"Make no mistake about it. There are still guys out there now that are very suspect. You've got to be careful. I still hear whispers and rumours. So if my saying something does some good — if it's only one person I help to be on guard — then I've got to take every opportunity to do that. Because if somebody had only mentioned to me, as a young kid . . . I mean, I don't know why I had to find myself in that situation before somebody said, 'Oh, you know, you don't want to go with that guy.' Why hadn't somebody told me that *before*?

"I'd like to see junior hockey held responsible for those awful things that went on back then — like the churches and the residential schools are being forced to be. It would be good to hear a public statement now and again, from somebody other than the victims. I would like to know that guys taken advantage of when they were just kids are getting the help they need today.

"And if anybody thinks I'm only saying this because Shaw and Finnan are dead, I want them to know that even if those sons of bitches were alive, I would say, 'Print it!' In fact, that's how it ended up in that Edmonton newspaper, where that guy who had been abused had the balls to call me up and say he appreciated me saying something. Because I said, 'Print it.'"

* * * * * * *

While some hockey fans remember Jim, many don't — a point I find peculiar at first, given that while Jim might not have been a Hall of Famer, he was not a minor leaguer either. He was a colourful character who had a 12-year career. A career in which he played for three "Original Six" teams, including the Leafs, hockey's highest-profiled club. He played with Bobby Orr and Wayne Gretzky, centered an all-star forward line between Bobby Hull and Gordie Howe, and participated in an international tournament against the Soviet Union's best. Plus he scored 10 points in a single game — a record matched only once, by Darryl Sittler. Jim also fought anybody and everybody, a pugilistic trait that normally endears a player to fans.

But then I consider how hockey churns out plenty of players, capitalizing on a large group of boys' hockey-playing dreams in such a way that it supports a small group of men's money-making desires. I realize that many, whose names I've not retained, have played the big-league game. Men like Joe Junkin, a goalie who played minor pro with Jim in the CHL in Oklahoma City, whose name I never would have known if not for Jim sharing it. Joe's 11-year hockey career — he played in 12 different cities in nine different leagues — more resembles that of Crash Davis, the journeyman catcher played by Kevin Costner in *Bull Durham*, than it does Ken Dryden.

I catch up with Junkin at his home in Harrisburg, Pennsylvania, where he's been laying carpet for 30 years. "I was playing Junior C in Bobcaygeon [Ontario] when my father died," Joe said. "And shortly after Dad passed away, some scout showed up at the door. He told me to sign a C-form, which basically meant I'd be a slave to one team for the rest of my life. But I was too scared to sign anything — I'd just lost my dad. So I was a free agent when I finally signed with Boston, and I think it was that freedom to move around that gave me a career."

"A career that one day took you to the NHL."

"Yup, for eight whopping minutes — December 14, 1968. We [the Bruins] were up 10-5 against Chicago. The game's almost over when Gerry Cheevers skates to the bench for what he said was equipment repairs. Then he tells [coach] Harry [Sinden], 'Why don't you put Joe in?' and I guess Harry figured, 'Sure, why not?'

"Then Cheevers tells me, 'Now listen, kid, you're going to have to watch for Bobby Hull. First thing he's going to do is whistle one up around your head to scare you and, after that, he'll start to bring them down a little at a time.' And that's exactly what Hull did. Cheevers told me later that he left that game because he didn't like facing Hull."[1]

The pride in Joe's voice is palpable. He's understandably pleased that someone might want to hear his story, but he's still got a fair share of humility. "Anyway, I'm sure you didn't call to talk about me.

"I remember Jimmy drove a red Corvette. Those were good times in Oklahoma City, where I hung around with all these guys from the prairies. They didn't like me at first, because I was from the East. Then all of a sudden we were playing Tulsa in the playoffs and it didn't matter anymore where anybody came from. We were in a war, and we were in it together.

"Tulsa had Brian Glennie on defence. Glennie was huge. And he and Jim got in a fight. They were going at it, hair flying everywhere. And Glennie landed three good shots to Jim's head, and Jim fell to his knees. We figured he was finished. But he pulled himself back up and kept throwing, and that motivated the whole team, that Jimmy would keep throwing punches at this big gorilla, long after most guys would have stayed down."

"You're expecting me to remember way back when?" Brian Glennie says after I ask what he might recall about his brief minor-league career. "Hah, I'm afraid I won't be of much help to you. I mean, I did have a cottage once in Fenelon Falls —" where I said Joe Junkin hailed from, and where I lived for more than a decade "—

1. Gregg Sheppard, who played with Junkin in Oklahoma City and Cheevers in Boston, tells this story differently — the classy Cheevers pulled himself from the game, (correctly) speculating that it was the popular Junkin's one and only opportunity to log NHL playing time.

it was on Sturgeon Point." This doesn't surprise me, what with Sturgeon Point being the only part of the Fenelon Falls district that has homes comparable in value to Brian's current Bracebridge, Ontario, abode.

"But if you think I can remember anything about playing in Tulsa, or any fight I had with Jim, you are sadly mistaken. I'm claiming concussion syndrome on this one," the University of Toronto psychology grad only half-jokes. "And I've got to tell you that was another time, many worlds away. Some days I ask myself, 'Did that really happen?' Like Team Canada '72. If I didn't still get fan mail from Europe, I wouldn't know whether I lived it or imagined it. It doesn't matter what you went on to do later in life. I was in the bar business, made a lot of money, lost it all when I made some bad decisions, and then made some of it back through the printing industry. And now I'm retired and doing charitable work, which is extremely satisfying. Yet I'll always be known as that guy who played hockey. It's like I'm stuck in some kind of time warp.

"I suppose I was more comfortable with it in my 20s, but now I don't see myself as being any different than anyone else. I'm just an old man with arthritis and a sore back. My back might not hurt quite like Jim's does, but, like Jim, my hockey career ended due to injuries and the resulting surgery.

"I can tell you I played in Tulsa because I didn't fit in, in Rochester, where Punch Imlach wanted me to play. Punch and I didn't see eye to eye. I'd just come off the Olympics where I'd played under Father David Bauer, and Father Bauer was brilliant. Suddenly there was this large generational difference between the old players in Rochester and me. I just wasn't comfortable there. So I told the Leafs that if they didn't send me to Tulsa I was going to be a phys. ed. teacher. But they did ship me out and that worked out well for me because Tulsa's where I played for Johnny McLellan, who went on to coach the Leafs."

Brian, not as interested as others in revisiting the past, works quickly to put my Tulsa inquiries to rest. "As for any fight I had with Jim," he insists, "I wasn't much of a fighter. That's not what I was there to do. I was out there to hit guys. I was strong, so I could take care of myself, but if I wanted to punch you, you'd see my swing coming from a long way away. I spent most of my fights just trying to make sure the other guy didn't get a good punch in.

"What I do remember from when I later played *with* Jim — in Toronto — is that he is a great guy and he had a wonderful gal."

Jim, when I later tell him I talked to Glennie: "It was a hundred degrees in Tulsa, and we did have a few fights. We were passing bennies — amphetamine tablets — around the dressing room. It was the first time I ever took an upper. I took one because we played the night before and it was so hot the rink was like water. I took that benny and I remember going to the faceoff circle and I couldn't line up properly. I put my stick about three feet away from where the puck would drop. I felt like I was jumping on a trampoline. It took a whole period before I could even skate. So I never, ever, took another benny. Because the one I had wasn't worth it.

"It was one of the toughest series I ever played in. We had a lot of small guys. Tulsa was running us and we were running them. The fans were nuts. And they had a couple of players besides Glennie that were tough. We had some tough guys on our team too. Guy Allen and Ross Lonsberry, for example — guys who could really handle themselves. So it wasn't just me out there. I think we won because we came ready to battle. I don't believe we actually cared if we won the hockey game. We just knew we wanted to win the war."

Then, for reasons of respect, Jim defers to Glennie. "Like Brian told you, he was never really a fighter, and I think that's why to this day he doesn't want to come across as one. But because he played rough and he could hit well, people wanted to fight him.

"I bet that's how he prided himself back then — not as a fighter but as a hard, tough player. I think that's pretty fair to him, because he could hit. That was his game. If you asked him about his greatest hits, he could probably rhyme off a few names in a few games where he nailed some pretty good hockey players. But fights? I'm not surprised he didn't want to talk about them.

"Brian was a big kid, so when he hit you, you knew it. So I decided if he was going to be running at us in these tiny little rinks where everything was slow because the ice was so bad, making it easier for him to hit guys, I'd have to send him a message that what he was doing was unacceptable. But what he and I did was just part of the intimidation game of those times, and while I don't remember the details of that fight with Brian as clearly as Joe does, I do remember I was awful sore after every game. But especially that game where I took that benny."

* * * * * * * *

Glen Bain, Saskatchewan's Bill Lesuk is an intense, deliberate speaker who closely examines every word he says to see if it is his best selection. It's not difficult to see how such a way of being might have helped the gifted scout to recognize talent for four NHL teams over 25 years, following a 13-year professional playing career that took him to five NHL cities, the WHA, and three minor-league stops. When I catch up with him at his Winnipeg home, I am curious to hear birddog Bill's assessment of Jim's minor-league career.

"Yes. I was there when Jim turned pro with the Central Hockey League's Oklahoma City Blazers," Bill recalls. "Plus, I played against, and with, Jim in junior. And from what I saw, the Jim Harrison who turned pro was exactly the same guy I saw suit up for Estevan. He was quite unassuming. It was always the team and his teammates first with Jimmy.

"But, holy Christ, here was a guy who played a very physical game and was of enormous value to his team both for his willingness to sacrifice his body and the considerable hockey skills he demonstrated. I never understood why so many NHL teams slotted him as a third-liner, because wherever he played, there were many nights when Jimmy was his team's MVP.

"Maybe it had something to do with the fact that if there was ever any trouble on the ice, you could bet Jimmy would be in the middle of it. Jim had this way of getting other people's respect. Not so much for himself, but for his team — kind of an Orland Kurtenbach type of player."

Bill is instinctively doing one of those things scouts do, when they compare an up-and-comer to another who played slightly before, but not entirely before, their subject's time. He is comparing Jim to another tough center from the prairies whose career — with the Bruins, Leafs, Rangers, and Canucks — played out mostly in the decade before Jim's did. "I'll tell you, when you played with Jimmy, you wanted him there when trouble broke out. And there are not many first-line centers you could say that about.

"I remember Jim showing up at his first pro training camp. In those days the veterans would show up overweight and need to play themselves into shape. Everyone knew you were not to hit the vets. But Jim couldn't play that way. This made him unpopular with the senior players. He's so competitive he didn't know how to hold back. I don't believe he'll ever know how. He's still a hard guy to tone down. Just look at the way he sticks up for retired guys, and how you can't slow him down even though he's had a tough time with his injuries and other things."

"He's right," Jim says with a sigh, when I tell him Bill Lesuk has described him as "a hard guy to tone down."

"Even before I turned pro with Oklahoma City, I was fighting against Boston management, which was crazy when I think about it now. I guess I didn't know any better. But I remember fighting for a $5,000 signing bonus because I wanted a Corvette and I knew one would cost me fifty-two hundred bucks. Guys who graduated junior a year ahead of me would come back to Estevan and tell us how management would give the guys from the East five thousand to sign, but the western boys only got twenty-five hundred. When I finally got the five grand, I went out and bought my car.

"Oklahoma City was where I really started to see the rivalry between eastern and western Canada, because if there was new equipment it went to the guys from the East, while we westerners got the used stuff. That's how cheap Bruins owner Weston Adams was, sending the big clubs' used underwear on to the minor-league guys. And everyone knew it was the western boys who were the reason we were winning. Even the guys from the East knew that, so after a while they wanted to hang out with us. But they couldn't understand how we could be out all night partying and then play as well as we did.

"Another cheap thing the Bruins did that never made any sense to me was, they never saw to it that their minor-league guys got good medical help. The club would hire doctors who were drunks. One was so bad he couldn't stop his hands from shaking. But he'd work for almost nothing, and that was all management cared about.

"This doctor would have to stitch our cuts, and the players wanted no part of that, so we'd tell the trainer to sew us up. In those days the trainer was the guy who sold pop. Some days he'd use black hockey tape to hold our cuts together. It's a wonder we didn't die of blood poisoning. The only way I'd get white tape was if I bought it myself, which I did sometimes. It was the same in other places. We'd say, 'Don't get cut in Fort Worth,' because we knew their doctor was a drunk.

"But mostly, that whole Oklahoma experience was great. We had a good team. There must have been 20 guys from that club that went on to the NHL. Barry Gibbs, Jim Lorentz, Tom Webster . . . And the fans were amazing. You'd never have known we were playing in a baseball town, because those people treated us like we were number one. The guys on that team appreciated what we had there. We used to get together all the time, and we stuck together.

"It was not like when you're in the big leagues and guys with families go their separate ways and some of the stars don't hang out with the rookies and the fringe players. No — none of us playing in the minors had any money to eat at restaurants, so we were always eating at each other's houses. Rookies never had to pay for a meal because the married guys and their wives were always having everyone over to their homes. They made sure no one was alone on a special occasion like Thanksgiving or Christmas. Bill and Mary Jane Lesuk were the leaders at that kind of thing. Mary Jane was like a mother hen to us all.

"The way that women like Mary Jane looked after us off-ice contributed to our on-ice success. And that club had a little success. That team had been good for a while — guys like Gerry Cheevers and Terry Crisp had played there. Then we had our good playoff run against Toronto's farm team in Tulsa. I always played well against them — that's why the Leafs later traded for me. Johnny McLellan told me that. He said the Leafs traded for me because they'd seen how good I played against their minor-league team.

"The Central league was a good league to play in, but the play was scrambled and disorganized. Coaching wasn't as good as in the NHL and neither were the players. NHL guys know how to give a pass and how to take one, and that makes everyone better and the game easier.

"You've probably seen how a guy can have better stats in the NHL than he had in the minors? How an average minor-leaguer suddenly looks like a superstar in the NHL? That's because the guys he's playing with, and the system he's playing in, make it easier for him. The hard part of the NHL game is the speed. A second here or there can make a world of difference.

"That year I played in Oklahoma City was one of my most enjoyable years in hockey. There I am, first time in the States — in Oklahoma no less, which was a perfect place for me because I'd always wanted to be a cowboy. I've got this big cowboy hat, I'm single, driving a Corvette, and hanging out with a great bunch of guys. Plus I've already played some games in the NHL so I'm feeling pretty good about my chances. Let's just say there was a lot of hoopla."

I was a season ticket holder for the Hamilton Canucks when they were the AHL [American Hockey League] affiliate for the parent Vancouver team. I thought the hockey talent was of high merit, but what I found noticeably missing from games was "star quality." There were lots of players in the minors willing to play tough, disciplined, positional hockey, banging the puck off the boards when pressured and forechecking tenaciously when the flow of the game called for it.

But for the most part, the game-changers were not present — they were in the NHL. The guys who could blow a game wide open. Or bring the spectators out of their seats because of some natural flash of athletic brilliance or colourful charisma. Those players may play in the minor leagues at some point on their journeys, but their skills are wanted in the big leagues, where the nation's affluent fee-paying clients await their creative cleverness.

This is especially true during periods of NHL expansion, when the talent pool is diluted to staff new rosters. So Jim didn't stay long in Oklahoma City — 43 regular-season games and another nine in the playoffs — before being summoned by the big club. But to suggest expansion played a significant role in creating an opening for Jim would be misleading. Yes, it's true the NHL had doubled in size the previous season, but the major-league lineup that Jim cracked was one of the best hockey teams of all time — the Big Bad Boston Bruins.

* * * * * * * *

I ask Jim to describe his first NHL goal, a milestone that many fans, regardless of age or athletic inability, dream of achieving.

"I know it was at Maple Leaf Gardens in Toronto on January 15, 1969," he rhymes off. "But other than that, I don't remember much about it. I think Johnny Bucyk and John McKenzie assisted on it." (They didn't.) "I still have the puck with the Leaf on it, but . . ." At this point Jim's interest in his own story fades. He glances at his watch, squirms in his seat, and winces when his back hurts.

"No, I can't tell you much about that first one. I'm not sure why that is, but I think it's because the big thrills for me in my rookie year came when I went into all those historic arenas like the Montreal Forum and the Detroit Olympia, and played against all those greats like Jean Beliveau and Terry Sawchuk. I was

49

mesmerized. Guys I'd dreamed of playing against, in rinks I'd only heard of. I remember those things really well. But my first goal? It was just another goal to me."

Wednesday, January 15, 1969[2]
At Maple Leaf Gardens

Boston 5, Toronto 5

Boston

Goal – 30 Cheevers, 1 Johnston

Defense – 4 Orr, 20 D. Smith, 26 Awrey, 6 Green, 10 R. Smith

Forwards – 7 Esposito, 8 Hodge, 28 Murphy, 17 Stanfield,
    9 Bucyk, 19 McKenzie, 21 Harrison, 14 Sather, 23 Shack,
    18 Westfall, 12 Cashman

Toronto

Goal – 30 Gamble, 1 Bower

Defense – 7 Horton, 23 Quinn, 8 Dorey, 4 Pelyk, 2 Pilote,
    3 Pronovost

Forwards – 9 Ullman, 19 Henderson, 14 Keon, 6 Ellis, 11 Oliver,
    16 Walton, 10 Armstrong, 27 Meehan, 15 Sutherland, 20
    Pulford

First Period

1. BOS Murphy 8 (Green, Esposito) 1:18
2. TOR Armstrong 4 (Dorey) 11:07
3. TOR Walton 12 (Henderson, Ullman) pp 16:34
4. BOS Hodge 18 (Green, Murphy) 18:36

---

2. Source: *The Hockey News*. With thanks to
sports.groups.yahoo.com/group/hockey_summary_project.

5. BOS Harrison 1 (Cashman, Westfall) 19:22
Penalties – Sutherland TOR (interference) 11:32; Cashman BOS
    (high-sticking) 15:03

Second Period
No scoring.
Penalties – Quinn TOR (hooking) 1:16; Quinn TOR
    (major-fighting) 5:26; Harrison BOS (major-fighting) 5:26;
    McKenzie BOS (tripping) 6:11; Sather BOS (cross-checking)
    8:25; Pilote TOR (tripping) 8:38

Third Period
6. TOR Walton 13 (Armstrong, Quinn) 3:24
7. BOS Esposito 26 (Cashman, Smith) pp 11:38
8. BOS McKenzie 13 (Green, Bucyk) 14:03
9. TOR Oliver 11 (Keon) 14:47
10. TOR Horton 5 (Sutherland, Henderson) 17:04
Penalties – Cheevers BOS (interference) served by Shack 3:35;
    Oliver TOR (interference) 9:41; Walton TOR (10-minute
    misconduct for pushing linesman) 14:03

Shots on goal

BOSTON	11	15	12	= 38
TORONTO	14	14	16	= 44

Goaltenders	Time	SA	GA	ENG	W/L/T
BOS Cheevers	60:00	44	5	0	T
TOR Gamble	60:00	38	5	0	T

But that season was not only about games against gods in
beatific buildings. After 16 games with the Bruins, Jim went back
to Oklahoma City, where injuries continued to plague him. First

he hurt his shoulder, and then he broke his hand fighting. Today, he laughs when recalling the suspension he received as a result of the fight. "They gave me a three-game suspension, but it didn't affect me because I was hurt, so I wouldn't have been playing anyway," he says.

He also suffered an eye injury. "A *serious* eye injury," Ross Lonsberry recalls. "One that required he spend two weeks in the hospital. It was so bad we thought he might lose sight in that eye. Yet as soon as he gets out, there he was with his face all bandaged up, insisting on racing some guy driving a GTO in Galveston, Texas. So here you have this rough-and-tough hockey player who's pretending he's a cowboy, until his Corvette starts fishtailing at 130 mph. At that point he went white as a ghost for what seemed like a week."

While the Montreal Canadiens would eventually eliminate the Blazers' parent Boston club and win the Stanley Cup, the 1968–69 NHL season had nonetheless proven productive for Jim and his employer, by bringing into being the Big Bad Boston Bruins and by drawing big-league attention to a ballsy newcomer named Harrison.

I was 10 years old when 1969 began. A scale model of an Apollo lunar module hung in my bedroom, thanks to my two older sisters, who suspended it from the ceiling using invisible thread. But because my myopic 10-year-old tendencies kept my attention on man's intention to walk on the moon, I was still 16 months away from discovering the game of hockey.

While many Canadian kids of that era were introduced to hockey well before the end of their first decade, my family did not feel compelled to advise me regarding the game. Not that I believe they made an intentional choice to hide hockey from me, but they wouldn't have wanted to relinquish the family television every Saturday night even if they had considered that I might enjoy the sport.

However, I realize now that while *my* imagination was locked on space travel, a robust Boston hockey club had begun to capture the attention of others. But that team was more than just sizable and sinful. Spearheaded by a 20-year-old Bobby Orr — I have no adjectives worthy of describing such a prodigy — that Bruin team was playing some amazing, high-scoring hockey.

Via a lineup that included star forwards Phil Esposito, Ken Hodge, and Derek Sanderson; journeymen Fred Stanfield, John McKenzie, and Ed Westfall; a solid defence corps led by the one-off Orr but supported by an extremely capable cast including Don Awrey, Gary Doak, and Dallas Smith; and a couple of big-game goaltenders in Gerry Cheevers and Eddie Johnston, this Bruin team was playing with a never-before-seen cocky confidence and, because of the presence of Orr, genius.

But, like successful teams in any era, that roster consisted not only of veteran players, but a nice blend of youngsters too. Players who, I have come to conclude via a talented sportswriter who worked those intoxicating times, brought injury relief and a boost of energy to this one-of-a-kind club.

Mark Mulvoy wrote in the February 3, 1969 edition of *Sports Illustrated*:

> The young players called up during the injury crisis, particularly Don Marcotte, Wayne Cashman, Rick Smith, and Jim Harrison, have performed like hardened Bruins. They have been rough and mean and not afraid to pick up penalties. Cashman started Boston to one victory when he smashed New York's Reggie Fleming with an elbow thrust. Smith has replaced Doak as the team's regular fifth defenseman. Harrison, who has been centering

Sanderson's line the last month, has been the most adventurous replacement of all.

Harrison wears his sideburns almost as long and thick as Sanderson and plays with the same disrespect for his elders. During his first shift in a game against the Canadiens in the Forum, Harrison successively ran at John Ferguson, Henri Richard, and Ted Harris. Harrison spent six minutes in the penalty box that night, but he so angered the Canadiens that they spent most of the game trying to retaliate and almost forgot about hockey. The Bruins won easily, and Harrison made the Montreal headlines.

Then last week in Detroit, the 21-year-old rookie confronted Gordie Howe — the man you do not challenge — and the Red Wings for the first time. Slam. He put Howe into the boards. Later they collided again, and this time Howe's stick fell to the ice. Harrison looked at it, paused, and then kicked it 30 feet down the ice. "He's what you'd call a disturber," says Milt Schmidt.

It must have been a very exciting time to be in Boston.

"It was. It *was* a very exciting time to be in Boston," Jim Lorentz says. Lorentz was another young center trying to crack that deep Bruins lineup. I asked for his take on what he, Harrison, and other young players would have witnessed. But, as with everyone I talk to on the phone, I try to determine where the Waterloo, Ontario–born and raised Lorentz is calling me from, because such information reveals much about a person. However, I'm not sure if it is because a career in public life has left Lorentz cautious — he was a Buffalo Sabres broadcaster for 26 years — or if it is the fanatic fly fisherman in him not wanting to give away the whereabouts of his favourite salmon rivers, but when I ask for his locale, Lorentz instructs me to say he is "about 45 minutes southwest of Miramachi, New Brunswick," and to "just leave it at that."

"As for that Boston experience, it was wonderful," he says. "I too had been playing in Oklahoma City when someone got injured on the big club and I got called up to fill in. They only played three lines in that era and that team was deep in talent so, like Jim, I was a fourth-line center — the kind of player who would fill in for Sanderson or Westfall when they had to miss the occasional shift because they were so frequently called on to kill penalties.

"Of course, I was too young to fully appreciate the experience. Even winning the Cup in '70 was tough for me to take in. But it wasn't hard to tell it was big for the city of Boston. It had been so long for those fans to wait between Cups, the parade was incredible. That team was the closest-knit club I ever played for, and I played for a tightly knit Sabres organization in the mid-'70s. But those Bruins had great chemistry, and those blue-collar fans loved that team."

That club also included another kind of player profile — the seasoned veteran that every great team has needed in the years before glory was achieved; the kind of guy who contributed to the early wins and collective attitude and had a history of winning elsewhere. But he is also the kind of man who is easily overlooked and forgotten because he gets asked to sit in the back while younger more capable hands bring the boat in — men like Ron Murphy, who played parts of five seasons with those Bruins, but, because of injuries, had to leave the game just when that team was getting great.

Born in 1933 in Hamilton, Murphy lives today in Nanticoke, Ontario. "A sleepy fishing village on the shore of Lake Erie," he tells me. "Nanticoke's mostly known for its nuclear power plant. The whole world seems to be worried about nuclear power — big deal! There's been nuclear power in Ontario for a long time and no one's ever died from it. If I were them, I'd be more worried about those windmills they're putting up everywhere. They sure cost a lot of money for the little amount of electricity they make."

Branded by management as cantankerous early in his playing career, and justifiably crotchety today — Murphy's in a wheelchair — I find his frankness refreshing. "When New York sent me to Chicago," he recalls, "they thought they were sending me to Siberia or something. They were trying to teach me a lesson, and then we won the Cup in '61. Hah, some lesson.

"Detroit thought the same thing when they traded me to Boston, and then Boston got real good. That just shows you the NHL can't keep you in the doldrums forever, even though that's what they try to do with lots of guys like me and your buddy . . . What's his name again?"

"Jim Harrison."

"He's from the West, right?"

"Uh-huh."

"My first memory of him is from Bruins training camp in London. He came in needing a haircut and driving a Corvette. A whole bunch of us piled into that car and he took us for a drive. I thought the front end was going to lift off the ground. Now, you may find that funny," Ron says when I liberate some genuine laughter. "But I'm telling you that when you got a car full of expensive talent like Espo and Hodgy, that's not the smartest thing to do, to go that fast. Imagine what would have been lost if that ship had gone down.

"That Bruins team got good because they traded for some great players, and then Orr arrived. I was there when he came up, and he made a difference right away.

"And I'm glad you remember me coaching your favourite junior team, but I don't have good memories of that time. I had 25 bosses in Kitchener and they all thought they knew more than I did. How is anyone supposed to win with 25 bosses? You say to me, 'Oh, you had a winning record with that team,' and I'm telling you, that wasn't winning as far as I'm concerned. If you call that winning, then you don't know much about winning. I only coached two guys in Kitchener who were good enough to go anywhere — Bill Barber and this big kid on defence named Larry . . . umm . . . Larry . . ."

"Robinson?"

"Yeah — Robinson. Those were the only two guys who were any good — Barber and Robinson.

"But getting back to that Boston team, I was probably close with 80 percent of the players on that club. That was a great bunch of guys. Just because I wasn't there when they won the Stanley Cup doesn't mean nothing. It just means I didn't play in the playoffs that year.

"People phone and ask me all the time what my best year was and things like that. Who cares? That was 50 years ago. Who expects me to remember back then? Look, some years were good and some were bad. That's life — the good goes with the bad. I know when I won, and I know what guys I won with. And the guys I won with know the same thing. So, really, who cares what the record books say?"

* * * * * * * * * *

Whenever I pick up a new hockey book, I scan the index to see if there are any references to any people or incidents that especially interest me — like in Phil Esposito's *Thunder and Lightning*, for example, where he shares an unsettling story about Jim. Admittedly, the items that grab my attention first usually involve some sex. I'm not proud of this preference, but it is the truth. The people who produce hockey for TV know this about me. They know that when I watch highlights, I'm titillated with the occasional insertion of an image of an ice girl or a comely female fan. Jim too intuitively knows this about me.

"Do you remember Tommy Williams?" he asks. We are in a hardware store. Jim is there to look at lumber, but he's seen that a saleswoman has caught *my* eye.

"For sure," I say. "Williams was an American player at a time when there were so few. Born in Minnesota somewhere, I think."

Jim grins. "I played with Tommy briefly in Boston. He was a good-looking guy — *really* good looking. Tommy was the kind of guy who had a girl in ever port and, wherever we went, they'd fall all over him. He was a classic."

Up to this point, Jim hasn't spoken much about the type of women who follow hockey players around on the road. Jim's more the kind of guy who dreams about owning enough land to raise alpacas, donkeys, and dogs than he does dating the dames. So I'm careful not to say anything that might cause him to change the subject, in case he has something else of a suggestive nature to say.

"Once, when I was with the Bruins, we went out drinking in New York and suddenly there were all these beautiful women around us. After a while, you'd begin to figure out that when they weren't with us, they were with baseball's Yankees. Someone would say, 'She's Mickey Mantle's girlfriend' . . . but they weren't going steady, if you know what I mean.

"There were always beautiful women around the mafia guys too, but it seemed the mob guys just wanted to hang out with us. The criminal element was everywhere. Organized crime guys like to hang with hockey players. So there was always gambling going on. Lots of guys lost a lot of money. This shouldn't surprise anybody. Several NHL teams have been owned by some really shady characters. I remember some clandestine things, like when I had to pass $10,000 in a paper bag, in an airport, to pay off another guy's gambling debt. I always saw myself as a pretty rough-and-tumble kind of guy, so I really liked the feeling of being around all those mafia guys and their girls, eating lobster all the time."

The Bruins celebrated the 40-year anniversary of their 1969–70 Cup win by holding a players' reunion. Bobby Orr told the Bruins they had to invite every guy who played on that team, not just the ones who got their name engraved on the Stanley Cup. That meant Jim was invited, and Caroline too. When the call came, Jim, used to having to scratch and claw for everything he gets from the NHL community, lightheartedly asked, "Are you sure you've got the right guy?"

"I bet you'd be surprised how many guys didn't show up," he later tells me. "We heard that Esposito said he wouldn't show if he didn't get paid an appearance fee. So it turned out the whole *family* wasn't there. Most of the guys who came were plumbers like me. Even Barry Wilkins showed up, and he's since succumbed to cancer.

"But I'll tell you, the Bruins couldn't have treated us any better. They put us up in a five-star hotel and made sure we had everything we needed. I think Caroline likes me better now. We mostly hung out with Bill Lesuk, Frank Spring, Rick Smith, and Wayne Carleton — the guy I got traded for.

"But because most of the big shots blew it off, the party was pretty subdued. Even the stars that did come didn't stay long — except for Eddie Johnston. Eddie stayed in our hotel and he organized so much for us, taking us all around Boston. Eddie's awesome."

Listening to Jim's joy, as he describes his time with old buddies, is an enjoyable moment for me. "One night, we all got talking about all the guys we played with in the minors, and I mentioned Joe Junkin, because I knew you'd been talking to him, and everybody smiled. You know, when you're in the middle of all that — when you're young and playing a game for a living — you don't appreciate playing with guys like Joe at the time. Like, by all rights, Joe shouldn't have even been playing at that level. But he was great, and everybody loved him. So everyone wanted to know what he was up to. Make sure, if you're talking to him again, you tell him.

I'm sure it would be great for Joe to know he was so highly thought of by the guys he played with."

"Tell me about Bobby," I ask, considering how number 4 had valued the plumbers' contribution to that Bruins team so much that, 40 years later, he would insist they all get an invitation to a party they might just as easily have missed.

"I first saw him when he was a kid in Oshawa and we were playing against him in the Memorial Cup. We knew his groin was hurting, so we hit him at every opportunity. But he still played unbelievable hockey.

"Then I didn't come up against him again until my first Bruins camp. That was when I saw he was a star through and through. He was only 19, but you could see the Howe in him — I imagine Crosby is the same way today. Those guys just know what's required of a star.

"Bobby was the perfect teammate. If you were at your first training camp, and he saw you eating all alone, he'd come and sit with you. He never gave the impression that he thought he was above anybody.

"The first time I was called up by the Bruins, my road roommate was Derek Sanderson, and later it was Glen Sather. Then management put me with Bobby. I think they put me with him because I wasn't playing much and the club figured it wouldn't make much difference if I was distracted by all the attention he was getting. The phone in our room would ring like crazy, and it wasn't me they were after. Some of the veterans would complain if they couldn't sleep before the game because of all the fuss over Bobby. But I was just thrilled to be tagging along with him.

"Later, in Chicago, we became close friends. We'd go fishing together. That was the biggest thrill for my mom, when she could sit at her kitchen table and have a coffee with Bobby Orr. But it all fell apart when I had my legal problems with Eagleson and Bobby was still loyal to Al. Then later it mostly mended itself.

"Man, was he humble. When a limousine would pick us up, Bobby would ride in the front with the driver because he never wanted to look like a big shot.

"But he was hurting. I'm talking about his knees, and the frustration that went along with that. I imagine that was the worst thing. Bobby could play through the physical pain a lot of the time, but not being able to do the things he knew he should be capable of doing at 28 — that was the worst of it.

"But he still played amazing hockey. When the team practiced, the place would be packed and people would be cheering for him to show them his magic. So he would just start ragging the puck, and when he did, no one could take it away from him. He just skated so much better than everyone else. And he'd do things he wouldn't try in a game because he never wanted to embarrass the other team. Today, lots of stars do their fancy tricks in games. That's one way that the game has changed. It's more about entertainment, but less respectful."

So that's what Jim's and my routine mostly looks like. I ask him to tell me his stories and he tells me what he's comfortable sharing. The part of that pattern that strikes me as precious comes when I think we're done. It's when I tell him I've got enough to go back to my desk with that his best stories come out. I'm not sure why — perhaps Jim is just warming up, maybe it's about trust, or maybe he's warming up to me — but whatever the reason, it's the content that comes after I've put my pen down that consistently captures my heart.

"Bobby paid for a lot of my late wife's medical bills when I couldn't, you know?" Jim says. "The alumni associations chipped in, but Bobby sent a large personal cheque. He didn't want anybody knowing he'd taken care of things for me when I couldn't. That's how humble he is. But I think people should know that Bobby took care of a lot of the bills that came from Liz's passing.

"I played with Gretzky a little and he was something. But Bobby's *my* hero. I feel very fortunate to have had him as a friend."

Twenty-three games into the 1969–70 season, Jim was traded to the Toronto Maple Leafs for winger Wayne Carleton. That's why I don't recall Jim as a Boston Bruin. Because, traded away December 10, 1969, Jim's Bruin career predates my first hockey memory of May 3, 1970.[3]

While I wouldn't have known any more about Wayne Carleton than I did Jim, I've since come to see that Wayne would have been worth watching. A year older than Jim, the Sudbury native played five years of Junior with the Toronto Marlboros, where Montreal scout Scotty Bowman compared him favourably to Guy Lafleur and Gilbert Perreault. Where, before eight knee surgeries slowed him down, Wayne played at an incredibly high level.

If I ever needed proof of Wayne's pedigree, I found it on Leafs TV in the form of old film footage where, as a 15-year-old, he was interviewed alongside a 13-year-old Bobby Orr by *Hockey Night in Canada*'s Ward Cornell.

In his Marlboro jacket and with a little wave in his hair, Wayne looked suave next to the brush-cut Bobby, whose massive, muscular legs already dominated such archived images. Both boys did a wonderful job of representing themselves and their respective junior clubs, and it was a joy to see and hear them speak at such an innocent time in their lives.

Because of the unique position Wayne indirectly played in Jim's past — after they were traded even-up for each other —

3. Boston was playing the St. Louis Blues in the first game of the Stanley Cup final. Bruins won the Cup seven days later on Bobby Orr's iconic goal, but my most vivid memory is from that first game — Blues goalie Jacques Plante suffered a concussion when a Fred Stanfield shot, deflected by Phil Esposito, hit Plante in the face, shattering his mask. Fifteen days later, Plante was traded to Harrison's Leafs.

I went in search of the retired financial planner and found him in Collingwood, Ontario, a Georgian Bay resort town where he's lived since 1969. I asked him what it was like to be traded from the last place Leafs to the eventual Cup-winning Bruins.

"It was great," Wayne says. "Not only because we won the Cup, but because I wanted out of Toronto. My relationship with Punch Imlach had not been good. I'd won the Memorial Cup with the Marlies in '64 when my wingers were Pete Stemkowski and Ron Ellis. Five years later, those guys were regulars in Toronto and, for whatever reason, Imlach saw me as not deserving of a job with the big club. It was always a personality thing with Punch. He and I just didn't get along, so it felt to me like he was trying to bury me in Rochester and Phoenix much of the time.

"I was rooming with Ronnie when the call came and, believe me, I was happy that it did. I had soured on the whole organization. I actually found my way to Boston that day, played the Rangers that night, and scored two goals. It wasn't long before [the] California [Golden Seals] claimed me in the Intra-League Draft — it was disappointing to have to leave such an impressive Boston club, but I have no regrets about getting out of Toronto. That's for sure."

So does that mean Jim was disappointed with being traded from the eventual Cup-winning Bruins to the last place Leafs? That's certainly the way it seemed to me, as a child, because I bought into all the bullshit about getting your name on the Stanley Cup being the greatest Canadian achievement ever. In fact, today it's not even about getting your name on the venerable trophy that's promoted. It's getting a Cup "ring" — an individual piece of jewellery that is better suited to being bragged about, shown off, or sold.

But just because the Bruins were on their way to their first Stanley Cup in 29 years there was no guarantee Jim would be part of it. Boston's lineup was deep at center and he wasn't the only young prospect competing for a chance to play. Today I consider how it might have made Jim happy to be traded to a team that saw him as part of the answer to what ailed them.

"Yes, it *was* good to get out of Boston," he says. "I know that must sound crazy, but things had gone terribly wrong for me there. I'd had a fight with some of my teammates. It was all alcohol-fuelled, but that's not an excuse. I'm just trying to tell you what it looked like at the time. I thought I might've been forgiven for what I did, but I wasn't. So it was never really comfortable for me in Boston after that.

"It started at a team meal. See, on days when there were no games, we'd go to practice and then we'd go out for something to eat and drink. We'd often have 10 or 12 beers, sometimes more. Then we'd go home and sleep it off. Anyway, at one of those team gatherings I said something stupid to Ken Hodge. I was not the only guy who had problems with Hodge, but I suppose it doesn't matter who started it — what I did was dumb.

"I was sitting beside Hodge and I asked him to pass the salt. He said, 'You got a broken arm? Get the salt yourself.' Then it got real bad real fast when, for no reason at all, I sucker-punched Gary Doak. And if you knew Doaky, you'd know he didn't deserve being treated like that. I've talked about it with guys like Cheevers since, and Cheesy told me that was a big mistake on my part, suckering Doaky. But sure enough, I did it.

"Phil Esposito tells this story in *his* book, but some of his details are different, because I believe Phil fabricated a few facts. I think he told this story in a way that made *him* look better, and me worse, for the benefit of his book. Don't get me wrong; what I did was stupid. But it didn't happen exactly as Esposito said it did. Phil made himself look like some kind of leader — some kind of peacekeeper — and he had me looking like I'd inflicted injuries on everybody and that I was a cancer in that dressing room. I was still a rookie, for Christ's sake. I couldn't have hurt that club if I'd wanted to.

"Anyway, the relationship between me and some of my team-mates was not good after that. And I'm the kind of guy, when I make a mistake it bothers me. That was a tough time for me. I didn't have a clue how to express my feelings in any kind of constructive way back then. I'm not sure I know how to now. Just ask poor Caroline. So I don't blame the players for being pissed off at me.

"And even though it starts out as something that's supposed to stay between the guys, you know that management eventually finds out. They just do, right? And I got traded when they did. So yeah, it would have been nice to be part of that Cup team if it had worked out, but I was actually glad to be traded to Toronto. It gave me a fresh start."

* * * * * * * * * *

As a child, I had greater affinity for my next-door neighbour than I did my father. After all, Mr. Gingerich and I had more in common. Of course, my need went deeper than that — I'm sure I was looking for a stronger relationship with a man than what my dad was up for. And quite possibly Mr. Gingerich, without a son himself, had his own reasons for giving me so much time and attention.

Today, it is easy to believe Mr. Gingerich must have had to occasionally create reasons to go into his house just to get away from me. But I'm sure he wasn't faking anything when, on May 3, 1970, he told me he was going inside to watch the Stanley Cup playoffs — game one of the Bruins vs. Blues final.

At which point, despite never having had any interest in sports, I went into my home to watch the same game as Mr. Gingerich.

And that was it: I was hooked. I experienced one of those epiphanies on which a life can turn. Seven days later I watched the final game of that series — that fateful day when Bobby flew. I then filled my summer reading hockey writers Jim Hunt, Frank Orr, and Gerald Eskenazi, and counting the days until the game returned.

By Thanksgiving, the Leafs were my team — an unfortunate choice over the long term, yet nothing short of ecstasy at the time. Goalies Plante and Parent were a dynamic duo; the defence consisted of Ley, Selwood, Pelyk, Dorey, McKenny, Baun, and Glennie; Keon was between Monahan and MacMillan; Ullman centered Henderson and Ellis; and Jim played with Armstrong and Sittler. I remember the other forwards as capable utility players: Spencer brought energy and toughness, Dupéré killed penalties, and Trottier popped the occasional timely goal. Today, I continue to remember every player's uniform number, yet despite watching the current Maple Leafs at least once every week, I can't recall the numbers worn by five.

I remember lying on our living room carpet, watching my Leafs on our new Zenith. Our family cat Joey was there watching my hamster Hilda while my mother sat on our uncomfortable green couch behind me. She'd be letting down hems and sewing on buttons, one eye on her stand-up ashtray and the other on me as I blathered on about how I couldn't understand why no one else in our house was as excited about this team as I was.

What was it about that hockey club that gave me such joy? It certainly wasn't a great team. At the start of the season, it was arguable whether it was even a good team. Not that the lineup didn't have some bright spots. Future Hall of Famers Keon and Ullman were creative, and Ellis and Henderson could clearly be counted on to contribute. But with an aging Armstrong, an unhappy Walton, an antiquated Plante, and an unpredictable Gamble, this team hardly seemed strong down the all-important middle. Plus there were questions about the club's inexperience.

Because, while the promise of youth can inspire hope and faith in some fans, a defence corps averaging less than 23 years of age tends to agitate old goalies.[4] Even two of the older forwards — Trottier and MacMillan — had only two games of NHL experience between them when that season began.

Yet, via the hypnotic superpower that Toronto's professional hockey teams have held over millions of Canadian boys and girls since 1917, this collection of athletes was to me as worthy of worship as any dynasty before or since — not in spite of its eclectic demographic mix, but because of it.

And no one captured my imagination more than Jim Harrison. Barely 23, Jim epitomized the NHL's new breed of full-sized center — the kind who could be counted on not only to score goals but also to pound on opponents. I was also aware that, in his role as a third-liner, Jim sacrificed ice time and fought foes on behalf of smaller teammates with different skills than him, a quality that even as a child I found engaging. Plus, Jim was a man. Not an ancient man like my father, who turned 43 in 1970, but a man much closer in age to my own generation than the one I had begun to reject.

Jim's appearance would also have played an important role in how I felt about him. Handsome enough to be offered modelling opportunities and product endorsements, Jim wore his hair stylishly long. Not that the length of his hair *then* would incite a reaction from anyone today. But by the standards of the time, in the slow-to-conform world of sports, the lengthiness of Jim's hair would be seen as a blatant act of rebellion. So, because Jim was a big, courageous, young man who acted defiantly, he was highly attractive to me, as was his modern-thinking adoption of a Scandinavian hockey stick, and his sexy number 7 fashionably

---

4. Veteran defenceman Bob Baun was acquired from St. Louis, for Brit Selby, on November 13, 1970, in a trade that stabilized the young defence, resulting in a considerably improved team and an eventual playoff spot.

displayed on the outside ankle of his ballistic nylon skates.

"Funny thing about that Finnish stick," says Jim, "is Carl Brewer was a distributor for Koho. So because Carl was such a good guy, I was giving one a try when I scored an overtime goal against Boston. Then, on CBC I got asked how I scored that goal, and I told all of Canada I scored because of that Koho — it was a silly thing to say, but I was nervous being on national TV. So Koho flew Liz and me to Finland and put us up in a beautiful place because of the publicity I got them. I used Koho from then on.

"But whether it was in Finland, Boston, Toronto . . . I was always a little overwhelmed by the attention in those days. I was quite shy back then — it made it difficult. Liz always told a story about going into Eaton's to buy a washer and dryer. She was so excited. We hadn't had one before. I was wearing some old jeans I'd gone duck hunting in the day before when the sales guy says, 'By the way, what do you do?' I said, 'I'm unemployed,' and my wife just rolled her eyes when he took us to the cheapest washing machines he had. I have no idea why I said that, but I know I didn't want to say I played hockey.

"In the end, Liz knew that some days I found all the attention hard to deal with, and she tried to keep me safe through it all. Liz was pretty special. Anybody that had met her saw that — even Eddie Shack. 'What are you doing with an idiot like that?' he'd ask her. Here was me, I couldn't walk, spaced out on painkillers half the time, and there's Shack trying to take advantage of that. I'll never forget it. It'll stick with me for the rest of my life. Yeah, she was such a unique person. She was quite an athlete herself — she rode equestrian. She was a very attractive lady. She went through a bad family thing with her dad beating her mom up, stuff like that, but it didn't slow her down. She carried me on her back for a few years, I'll tell you."

Jim suddenly recalls me saying that, as a child, I'd found the number 7 he wore highly attractive. "Most of us didn't get a choice what number we wore," he explains. "They just gave you whatever number they wanted, and you were lucky to have it. But the reason I switched from number 12 to 7 was that Tim Horton wore number 7 when I arrived in Toronto, but when Tim was traded, Keon and Armstrong decided there had to be this big presentation to me at practice, of number 7. Because it had been Max Bentley's number when he played for the Leafs in the '40s. The thing about Bentley was, he'd been one of the best stick-handlers ever, and as Keon and Armstrong liked to point out whenever they had an audience, I had a reputation for being one of the worst stick-handlers of all time. So those jackasses thought it would be funny if I wore number 7. That's when everybody started calling me Max."

I remember listening to Dave Keon's one and only hockey fight on CKFH, my portable transistor radio tucked tightly under my official NHL bedsheets. Davey's sparring partner that night was Penguin Gregg Sheppard.

"You're right. I did fight with Dave Keon. It was Keon's only major penalty, ever," Gregg says when I catch up with him at his North Battleford, Saskatchewan, home. I'd called to talk about Gregg's time with Jim in junior, but we'd gotten sidetracked. "Davey was one of my favourite players growing up," Gregg says, "him and Dick Duff.

"But another little-known story about Keon and me happened when we both finished our playing careers on the same night, against each other. Davey was back in the NHL with Hartford after playing in the WHA, and I was with Pittsburgh. It was the last game of the year and we were both playing our final shifts. So I skated over to him and I don't know what he thought I was going to do — maybe he thought I wanted to fight him again — but I just grabbed his stick right out of his hands. I said, 'You aren't going to need this anymore,' and I headed back to our bench.

I just wanted the stick that Dave Keon used on his last shift in his final game. I never stuck around long enough to see what his reaction was, but I still have that stick."

"I have been thinking about that Leaf/Flyer game you showed me the other night, from '71," Jim says with a hint of sorrow. "There's a scene where Brian Spencer puts his arm around me on the bench. Spencer was a troubled kid — even in junior. First time I met him he was playing for the Calgary Centennials, and you could see then he was a nutcase. Another time, he called me out back to show me something he had in the trunk of his car — he had 10 skinned cats. Somebody's pets, probably. If I hadn't already figured it out, that was all the proof I needed to see Spinner was a little screwy. When he fought, his eyes would roll back into the top of his head, so all you could see of them was white.

"Plus, he carried a handgun. We used to try to get food to his child, because he was spending all his money on army stuff. He'd spit on that kid when it wouldn't stop crying. There was something seriously wrong with Brian. It obviously showed up in the end when he got himself shot in Florida.

"When he played for Long Island he built a big army truck and equipped it with machine guns. Then once he got into drugs, you knew something was going to happen. Playing in the States is a whole different lifestyle. In Toronto we all looked after him, but when he went to other cities he got into other things. Sad story, Spencer was. His dad went into a TV station in northern B.C. with a gun when he learned they weren't going to broadcast his son's game, and the cops had to kill him."

Jim takes a reflective inventory of the players in that game from '71. "Wayne Hillman died way too young too," he says. "Not like Spencer, but I was thinking about Wayne because he was in that

Philadelphia game. I played with him in Cleveland. He looked after us, always organized card games, made sure the bar was set up. Because I didn't play cards, I mostly drank. I drank for the guys who did play cards, and I drank for the guys who didn't show up. Wayne was a great guy. I think he had a heart attack.

"Larry Hale used to work at my hockey schools. He's in Penticton now. Very close to his mother, he always had something funny to say about her. I remember those stories more than I do the goals I scored.

"Seeing Garry Monahan reminded me of how we used to tease him that he didn't know how to fight. Nobody likes to be told they're not tough, but Garry was very studious. He would know what was going to happen with mortgages, and I was too stupid to care. He's been dating a woman from Vancouver who has a daughter in Kelowna, so we've been getting together now and then, but I haven't talked to him in a couple of months. He had a successful career in real estate after he quit playing.

"Both our wives died from cancer," Jim adds quietly. "There were maybe eight ladies off that Leaf team that suffered from cancer. Ballard made a wives' room for them. Who knows what he might have put in there — they used all kinds of chemicals in those days. That's quite a few women to suffer at the same time — a third of the roster.

"Joe Watson played in Estevan before I did," he says, getting back to the players. "We used to meet at a hockey school in Smithers, B.C. I played fastball with Joe Sgro, our trainer, and Matt Pavelich, one of the linesmen in that game.

"When you're young you're going 90 miles an hour, but the veterans know better. They've figured out they don't have to go like hell. Guys like George Armstrong — he was such a great backchecker, saving my bacon many a night. He knew to get back, but he also knew not to skate around like a fool.

"Bruce Gamble's dead. He had a heart attack too. There are lots of stories about Bruce and beer, but my favourite is about the time he went out and bought 30 hamburgers for everybody. Good team-man. We didn't have much money, so, when you're playing on the road in St. Louis and your teammate buys burgers for everybody like that — that was a nice gesture from Bruce that I've obviously never forgotten.

"I got a kick out of hearing Paul Henderson call for a line change as he headed for the bench. He was trying to get off and he wanted whoever was next — probably Spencer — to know. Paul's shifts were short. He would skate like hell and then get off. We were all supposed to do that, but not everyone did. It's been a long time, but I still recognized Paul's voice when I heard him call out like that.

"It would have been good to see Bernie Parent play in that game. Goaltenders were off the wall in that era. Some were grumpy. Others had girlfriends who ran the show. It's a tough position, but I loved putting on the pads at practice, every chance I could. It never occurred to me that if I bust an ankle, that'd be it for me.

"My career could have ended quickly, just because I wanted to pretend I was Gerry Cheevers for an hour or two. Gerry was the best goalie I ever played with. Best I ever played *against* was Ken Dryden. He was just so big. Sawchuk was great, Plante was good. Tony Esposito was incredible. Johnny Bower was amazing. He still practiced with us for two or three years after he retired. I couldn't score on him. Glenn Hall, another good one.

"Scoring 19 [in 1971–72] was quite an achievement for me. Scoring 19 goals playing behind Keon and Ullman? Those two guys used to get a lot of ice time, understandably. Everybody thought my back was good then, but it wasn't. I might have scored 40 goals if it had been.

"I laughed when I saw Jim Dorey on defence. We called him 'Flipper,' but I don't remember why. It was fun to watch that game with you.

"Oh yeah, what I meant to say was: Spencer had troubles but he was still a teammate, so we all stuck up for each other. I thought of that when I saw him put his arm around me, because Spinner's story was a sad one."

Live Kitchener Ranger games, televised junior hockey out of Hamilton, Sabre contests via a cross-border Buffalo station, Sunday-afternoon American network games, and the Leafs to love twice a week. I believed the world was mine for the taking, even though — or perhaps because — all that indulgence rendered school work an easy afterthought.

"Yes, I certainly understand what you mean when you say, 'School work was an afterthought,'" Jim Dorey tells me from his office in his hometown of Kingston, Ontario, where he works at brokering big insurance matters, a line of employment that has rewarded him throughout his post-hockey playing days. "That's pretty much the story of *my* childhood. I paid lip service to all the things that were supposed to be important — things like school. But really, hockey was the only thing that mattered to me."

There is considerable spirit in how Dorey speaks. A square-jawed, handsome man his entire life, he's hung on to not only his good looks, but a lot of lucid memories. "As far back as I can remember," he says, "my world was turning fast. I was always playing with guys who were older than I was. That's the way it was on outdoor rinks. You're playing with older kids, so if you're not going full speed and playing as aggressively as you can, you'll find yourself sitting in a snowbank.

"Then it just gets faster — bantam, midget, junior, getting to the Toronto Maple Leafs. And you better be ready to go when you get there, or you won't be staying for long. I can tell you, it's tough.

"Everything was so fast, it made it difficult to appreciate it while you were in it. Here's the best way I can describe it: about 10 or 12 years ago, I was travelling with the Legends of Hockey, playing old-timer games with guys like Guy Lafleur and Gilbert Perreault. We were playing in some small town on the top of Newfoundland in a rink where, when you step out the door and look north, the next stop is the Arctic. This rink was meant to hold about twelve hundred people, yet they'd packed in what felt like five thousand. People were piled eight or nine deep, right along the boards, and I mean packed in, tight.

"And why? So they can get a glimpse of some guy who played pro hockey. It was amazing when I actually thought about it. And that's what I did — I thought about it. I'm handling the puck along the boards and I look into the stands and see all these Newfoundlanders looking back at me.

"Next thing you know I've got tears in my eyes and my heart started to drop," the former tough guy tries to tell me. "Look, I don't share this story with just anybody, but you're a writer, see what you can do with it. The entire experience was a good wake-up call for me. All these people, in their own way, were telling me how fortunate I was, and still am, and that sometimes I lose sight of that, given the speed at which life travels."

Dorey works hard to emotionally explore what is, for many men, uncharted territory: "I can tell you, it's tough. The entire country's eyes are on you the whole way — the people and the press. Not that we didn't have fun. In fact, that's how I remember Jimmy. Not so much for any closeness I felt for him off the ice, but for what it meant to be his teammate, in games, at practice, and on the road. We both had our quirks. So I thought Jim was a real fun guy to be around. That being said, you'd have to say we shared some kind of mutual respect as well. I'm sure we both knew the other guy didn't have a problem with rubbing out someone on the other team if that's what it came down to.

"But players weren't so guarded then. We gathered as guys and shared beer, sandwiches, and comradeship. So, yeah, playing with Jimmy, for the Toronto Maple Leafs of your youth, was a lot of fun for me. I just don't know where it all went, and why it had to go so fast."

* * * * * * * * * * *

Jim didn't enjoy Jacques Plante, and I found this funny in an awkward sort of way because, at 11, I revered Jake the Snake. Playing street hockey, if I wasn't Jim Harrison, I was Jacques Plante. Yet, the way Jim ranted on, I couldn't bring myself to tell him about the crush I had on the late great goalie. Silly, I know, but I toss Jacques's name out for discussion, hoping to hear more about that Toronto team that meant so much to me, and Jim pounces on Plante like a chicken on a June bug. "Jacques Plante was an idiot. Me, me, me — that's what Plante was. A bunch of guys overheard him from their hotel rooms. He was in the hallway telling Stafford Smythe, the team owner — who was drunk — how great *he* [Plante] was and how the rest of us were a bunch of slackers," Jim says, shaking his head at the thought of such disloyalty. "So we took a bunch of furniture from the lobby and piled it up against Plante's hotel room door. Then he didn't want to stay in the same hotel as the rest of us anymore. He said we were too loud for him."

I wonder if it was generational — Plante was 20 years older than Jim. "No," he insists. "It wasn't. I didn't like him because he wasn't a team player. But you're right to ask about age because, back then, it was tough to be part of an older team in the short time after you arrived. Veterans wouldn't let the young guys drink with them until they'd earned their stripes. It didn't take me long before the Leaf vets accepted me, but it didn't happen right away. Even when they did let me in, it was partly because I drank beer. Rye whisky was out. That's how dumb we were. We used to think that beer replenished you and booze depleted you.

"If the veterans got something on you — something they could needle you about — they were relentless. Like when they figured out Rick Ley had a temper, guys would push his buttons every chance they got.

"The veterans ruled in Toronto," Jim continues. "The Leafs and the Canadiens had reputations for being that way in those days. More than other clubs, Leaf and Hab veterans would make things hard for the young guys if they were different.

"There was something odd about some of Toronto's fans too. Guys who hunt would want us along — big-shot Ontario guys who liked to hang out with hockey players. That was one of the strange things about Toronto people — they didn't care if you were a good person or not, but if you were a hockey player they wanted to hang out with you. I remember Darryl Sittler and I went with some of them to St. Thomas, near London. These guys used hounds to chase rabbits into the open, where the so-called hunter could pop that rabbit as it ran by. I grew up hunting and fishing, but chasing rabbits with dogs is not a sport to me. I'd see the rabbit go by and just let it go. Then these Ontario guys would say, 'Didn't that rabbit cross your trail?' and I'd say, 'Hmm, I must have missed him.'

"Another time Darryl, Bernie Parent, and I went ice fishing on Lake Simcoe. We got caught in a storm and couldn't get off the ice at the end of the day, so we slept in the hut. We had a game the next day and we made it, but we missed the morning skate. I remember Leafs general manager Jim Gregory fining us each five hundred bucks. I was only making eleven grand. I think he gave that money back to me when I scored two goals that night, but, knowing how cheap Harold Ballard was, that doesn't sound quite right, does it? That's the only time I scored two goals in an NHL game. Guilt's a good motivator."

Those were the good days with Darryl. "When I left Toronto, I lost some of my friendship with Darryl and his wife, Wendy. I found that sad. At one point, Darryl and I had roomed together. But once you leave a team, your friendships deteriorate. Then I heard Ballard wanted me back in Toronto when I jumped from the World Hockey in '76, but something happened. The story got back to me that Darryl said he didn't think I could help the Toronto Maple Leafs.

"That was always a sore point with me because I would have liked to have gone back to Toronto. My wife lived there, we had a farm there, but that was the story I heard. I don't know for sure if that story is true, but a couple of reliable sources said that Darryl didn't want me back in Toronto.

"Some people suggested I may have been a threat to him at center," Jim recalls, "but I would never have been a threat to *him*. I would have been a complement to him. I think I could have helped them. But at that time they had 12 or 13 Eagleson clients on that team, and Darryl was pretty much running the hockey club. So our friendship, especially after the Eagleson thing blew up, never recovered. We've not talked since.

"To be truthful, I can't forgive him for being friends with Eagleson. Because I don't think anybody should be a friend to Eagleson after what he did to hockey players. If they are, well, they don't have my friendship. Darryl may not want my friendship, but that is probably the worst thing I can say about any hockey player — that if they choose to be friends with Eagleson after what he did to hockey players, then they don't have the respect of anyone except those like them.

"There are many players that Eagleson took advantage of, and Darryl knows this too. So I have trouble understanding how Darryl can say that Eagleson is a good friend. I don't get it myself, but obviously other guys feel differently.

"Any way you look at it," Jim concludes, "it's unfortunate what happened with Darryl and me. We were really close. I used to look after him when he broke in with the Leafs. That's the way it goes, I guess."

It was while playing for Toronto in 1969 that Jim met Liz. "Her dad might not have been keen on her choice of husband, but Liz's attitude was, 'Too bad if Dad doesn't like him,'" Nora Kunopaski tells me from her home in Aurora, Ontario. "So it didn't matter what Jim did. Liz accepted and forgave him." Former neighbours, Nora and her husband, Tony, used to hang out with the Harrisons.

"That's just Jim doing what he does, Liz would say. I remember once, she had planned this big birthday party for him. Everyone was there, sitting around waiting for him to return home. There was tension, because he was late and nobody knew where he was. Then he walked in the house and took off his jacket and, otherwise clothed, he dove into the pool with the kids. Suddenly, whatever tension existed was gone.

"Those were fun times — we made many wonderful memories. Jim and Tony used to call us 'the damage sisters' because of the economic devastation we inflicted with our credit cards. But Liz and I were much more than just shopping buddies. We were more like sisters than friends, spending Christmases together and travelling to Florida and the Bahamas. Those years with Liz were fun, whether taking our kids to school or to skate, we laughed so hard some days my sides would hurt."

Nora's recollection changes direction. "Liz wanted so badly to beat that illness she had. Her mother died of the same disease. We had mutual friends, Barb and Garry [Monahan, of the Leafs], who Liz supported when Barb took ill from the same sickness.

"I remember calling Liz on her 50th birthday. She asked if I could come to Kelowna to help her plan her funeral. Jim just couldn't talk about funeral arrangements. It was too difficult for him to accept. I know it bothered Liz that she couldn't fix Jim's problems with hockey — that she left that business unfinished — because she was beside him the whole way. She wanted to see him get what she believed was rightfully his."

Jim: "More than anyone, Nora saw what Liz and I went through with my injuries and the Players' Association. Nora saw the times I couldn't walk, and she saw how Liz took control when I wasn't able to.

"A lot of our friends knew that we gave up things we couldn't do as a family because of my injuries — like how we had to sell our farm because I couldn't do the work. All that went down when Eagleson was still running things, and everyone thought I was the guy in the wrong. Everybody said that the Players' Association was doing everything it was supposed to, that Eagleson was doing everything he could, and that it was just me, sour grapes.

"But if Al — my agent and player rep — had managed me the way he should have, I might still have my farm today — a piece of property that's probably worth about $20 million now. So you can look at it and say, 'Hey, hindsight, things happen,' but if you had a piece of property on top of Toronto like we did, it's worth a few bucks today.

"I know you wanted to talk about the Leafs," Jim says, "but it's hard for me not to go to some sad places when I talk about my time in Toronto. Sorry about that. But that's the thing — I didn't just lose my money and my health. Some of my best friends disappeared too."

Born in 1933, Alan Eagleson was a card-carrying Progressive Conservative when, in the early '70s, he caught the attention of many Canadians, mostly as Bobby Orr's agent, the founding head of the NHL Players' Association, and the primary force behind the 1972 Soviet Summit Series. That's when I noticed him. I saw Eagleson as the man in the middle of Canada's Series of the Century.

I was 13 that summer of '72 when I learned some tickets to the Canadian portion of that epic battle were to be distributed via a lottery. I'll never forget the day our mailman delivered a letter telling me about two grey seats I'd won the right to purchase for game two in Toronto — I sat in the second-to-last row with my oldest sister, Wendy.

But it was game seven where I first took note of Eagleson. I remember him being escorted across the ice in Moscow — with both hands extended in the air, giving the Russians the finger — after trouble broke out in the section where he'd been seated. In that moment, as a child caught up in the Cold War, I was in the same emotional state the majority of Canadians were: it was us against them.

But today, as an adult, I remember that iconic moment with little sentiment. Now I wonder what entitlement and power a man must believe he possesses, and what gall he must have, to stand on Russian soil in the middle of an enormous, hostile crowd and tell an entire Communist country, their leadership regime, and their powerful army to fuck off.

* * * * * * * * * * * *

When Dale Hoganson and Jim Harrison met as kids in Estevan in 1964, they couldn't have comprehended what enormous change lay ahead for hockey. After decades of club-sponsored junior teams, the NHL created an Amateur Draft whereby graduating players could be dispersed within an equitable system.

Dale was part of that first draft, chosen 16th overall by the Los Angeles Kings. "I wasn't happy about that," he says when I speak with him at his Saskatchewan home. "I played at a good time, but a strange time. Guys in Estevan had always gone from junior to Oklahoma City and, if they were good enough, on to the Bruins. I was the first to not go that route. I didn't like that at the beginning, because in Oklahoma City you'd know half the team when you got there. Then I figured out it was good in a way, because Boston had so much talent I wasn't going to get to play there. But in Los Angeles I was. Then along came the World Hockey Association and more strange times."

I committed myself during the summer of '72 to refusing to pass into puberty, and hockey was my ticket to denial. I noticed when my neighbour wore a pin on his plaid suit jacket that read, "To Russia with Hull or to Hull with Russia." Bobby Hull had been denied the opportunity to play in the upcoming Canada-Russia series because he had the supposed audacity to sign a million-dollar contract to play in a rival league — in an era when $100,000 was considered a ridiculous amount to pay an athlete. The NHL was sending a message: there was a price to be paid for leaving.

I was so caught up in the hype of the day that I would have been disappointed had that series not been played. Like the majority of Canadians, I naively believed that talented team would not notice the absence of Hull. And while I was old enough to feel indignant about the senior league's snub of one of hockey's greats, I was too young to understand the enormous economics of it all.

Yet, to a child like me, the signing of Bobby Hull gave the WHA exactly what it had hoped to achieve — instant credibility. I have no recollection of believing, at any point during the league's seven-season existence, that the WHA iced an inferior game. To me, it was another NHL.

True, I initially felt shock as I watched the new teams ravage my beloved Leaf lineup — a process as easy as shooting fish in a barrel, given owner Harold Ballard's tight-fisted refusal to take the maverick league seriously. But my grief was short lived, as I quickly learned to follow the stars of the WHA.

"What was I going to do?" Dale asks. "I'd been traded by Los Angeles to Montreal. On one hand, it was great going to such a good team. But I wasn't going to play much in Montreal. I was either going to make no money in the minors or go to the WHA. It was a no-brainer to me.

"I was making $29,000 a year playing in the NHL, where I was rooming with one of the all-time greatest players — Henri Richard — and he was making fifty-seven thou. Then the WHA comes along and offers me $90,000 a year for three years, plus a $90,000 signing bonus. Even the [NHL's] Atlanta Flames were willing to give me fifty thou.

"The WHA was a good league. The players knew that. The NHL maybe had three good lines, and the WHA had two. Remember, I stayed with Quebec when they came into the NHL with Edmonton, Hartford, and Winnipeg. And you know what? The calibre of play was not much different. It couldn't have been or those four teams wouldn't have done so well, and they were all strong teams when they joined the NHL.

"Right away we played some great games against Montreal. We had such a rivalry. I remember the guy from the Quebec waterworks saying he could tell when the first period of a Montreal-Quebec playoff game was over, because the water level would drop by two feet when everyone in the province got up to go for a piss at the same time. The WHA was a good league, and there were days when Jim Harrison was the best player in the WHA."

Days like January 30, 1973, when Jim scored 10 points in a single game — a big-league record that's never been beaten and only tied on one other occasion (Darryl Sittler, Toronto vs. Boston, February 7, 1976).

Alberta Oilers 11, New York Raiders 3
At Edmonton Gardens

First Period

1. ALB Harrison 19 (Carlin, Patenaude) 4:48
2. ALB Fonteyne 7 (Hamilton, Harrison) 5:40
3. NY Peacosh 23 (Sheehan, Ward) 7:47
4. ALB Hamilton 6 (Harrison, Wall) 11:05
5. NY Kennedy 4 (Perry, Willis) 12:43

Second Period

6. ALB Wall 7 (Hicke, Harrison) 13:25
7. ALB Harrison 20 (Barrie, Fonteyne) 15:38

Third Period

8. ALB Carlyle 3 (Harrison, Barrie) 5:06
9. ALB Blanchette 5 (Harrison, Barrie) 7:43
10. ALB Patenaude 16 (Baird) 10:48
11. ALB Barrie 6 (Fontaine, Harrison) 11:40
12. ALB Carlyle 4 (Harrison, Barrie) 12:00
13. ALB Harrison 21 (Blanchette, Wall) 12:33
14. NY Laughton 16 (Kennedy) 17:49

Shots on goal

NEW YORK	10	6	4	= 20
ALBERTA	11	18	23	= 52

5. Source: *The Complete Historical & Statistical Reference to the World Hockey Association 1972–79*, 8th edition, by Scott Surgent. With thanks to sports.groups.yahoo.com/group/hockey_summary_project.

Goaltenders

| NY | Ian Wilkie and Gary Kurt |
| ALB | Jack Norris |

But just as he doesn't recall his first NHL goal, Jim remembers little about the specifics of this game. I ask him why he thinks that is.

"We had another game to get to," he says. "In those days, we played some double-headers — back-to-back games on consecutive nights or afternoons — to cut down on travel costs. So a lot of the detail regarding that game is just a blur to me today. I do remember I missed three breakaways that night. Any injuries I might have been suffering from were not bothering me that game." Jim laughs. "I believed I was the fastest skater in the world that night. The puck seemed to follow me around and I was able to pass and shoot at will.

"A lot of people don't remember that game. Until the [NFL's] Miami Dolphins beat me out for the Wilkinson Sword Award [honouring 1973's biggest sporting achievement], few people gave my game a second thought. Until I came in second to [Larry] Csonka, [Jim] Kiick, and [Paul] Warfield when their team went undefeated, my big game hadn't caught anybody's attention. I didn't even think about it much until then, though I did keep that stick for some reason, but it sat in a closet for the longest time. Then my game was put in the *Guinness Book of World Records*. My kids got a kick out of that, of course."

I study the game summary. "One of the goalies was Kitchener's Gary Kurt."

"Edmonton's Ian Wilkie was the other," Jim recalls. "Jack Norris was in goal for us. He's a grain farmer in Delisle, Saskatchewan. He was a good goalie. Delisle is famous for being where the Bentley brothers come from — Max and Doug. Jack has a huge ranch, one of the biggest in Canada. Sometimes we'd have 10 or 15 guys come up to Jack's and we'd all shoot ducks outside of Saskatoon. We'd go there in August and I'd help him drive the combine. Then he had a brain aneurism while playing old-timers' hockey. He passed out and nobody could tell why."

Fascinated with what I've just learned about Jack, and a fan of game summaries, I desire additional detail about other players who figured into the Oilers' scoring that magical night. So I read aloud last names and Jim filled in further facts.

"Barrie?"

"Doug. Doug was a tough kid. One of the toughest in junior hockey, but when he got to the NHL, all those heavyweights took over on him. But he didn't back down. He played in Buffalo. I think Dougie has got a sporting-goods store south of Edmonton, north of Red Deer — Wetaskiwin maybe. I played with him at the Memorial Cup in Oshawa."

"Hamilton?"

"No, Oshawa."

"Hah — no, I mean the *player* Hamilton."

"Oh. Al. He was captain of that Memorial Cup team I went with. His Oiler number is retired. He was 'Mr. Edmonton Hockey' for a long time. Some shifts, in that New York game, I played with defencemen on my wing. Al and Doug were those defencemen."

Jim's having fun. "Brian Carlin and Rusty Patenaude played for that team too. Brian owns one of the biggest real estate agencies in Canada. The coaches, I think, were Ray Kinasewich and Glenn Hall. But Bill Hunter fired Ray partway through the season. I don't know if it was before that game or shortly afterwards. Whoever was coaching double-shifted me, so I played with all kinds of guys that night. The next year Brian Shaw — the pedophile — was hired to coach.

"Me, Rusty Patenaude, his wife, Hazel, and my wife, Liz, were good friends. Hazel supported Liz through her sickness. But when Liz was dying, Hazel didn't get a call to tell her, so she wasn't there at the end. It never occurred to me that Hazel might get missed. Because when you're at the hospital and the funeral home, those kinds of things are all a blur. But I wish that Hazel hadn't been forgotten. I felt bad. Still do."

When Jim gets talking about his playing days, it's not uncommon for him to revisit his grief regarding Liz — she was there the entire way. My approach to his show of emotion is to give him room, until he sends me a signal that he's ready to go on.

"Who else you got there?" he eventually asks.

"Wall."

"Bob — he's a good guy. He owns a Tim Hortons in Aurora. He always put the puck right on my stick — never in my feet. He was so underrated when he played for Detroit. Then he came to play with us, and he was like Doug Harvey. He wasn't flashy, and often you wouldn't even know he was there, but he was great. Bob had a heart attack. I hope he's well. Nice wife, nice kids."

"Hicke?" I ask, knowing there were two Hicke brothers but not knowing which one Jim played with that night.

"Billy — he was a real classy guy. You could tell he'd played for the Canadiens. He died from pancreatic cancer. I played junior against his brother. Holy Christ, Ernie was tough. When you play in Montreal, you've got to be accepted by the fans. But because Billy wasn't the best of skaters, they didn't appreciate him. It didn't help that he wasn't French.

"We used to always laugh on the bench when Billy would get a breakaway, and we'd wonder if he was going to make it. He always looked like he was skating on gravel. He was older than a lot of us, and the coaches didn't like him because he was always overweight. A coach like Brian Shaw wouldn't have a clue what a winner was.

"Hicke could hold court," Jim continues. "We all wanted to know what it was like to be a Montreal Canadien. In those days, if you were seen talking to guys on other teams, even at a hockey school, you were fired, hated, or something else. Suddenly the WHA was happening and we had an option. Some great stories were coming out.

"One of the first things guys would ask Billy was what the Canadiens' training camps were like in their Stanley Cup days. So we'd have a few beers and Billy just had a great way of telling stories. His wife was really nice too. There are just people you can tell have won Stanley Cups.

"Billy owned the Regina Pats when I coached in Moose Jaw. Then, because there are a lot of political things that go on in hockey, suddenly I'm not only coaching but I'm running the show for a couple of months. We knew Theo Fleury was leaving and the team wasn't doing very well. So I decided I was going to trade Fleury to Regina because Regina had a shot at the Memorial Cup, and we needed more guys who could make us better.

"Billy and I made a deal over a bottle of rum. Then ownership got word that I was going to trade Fleury, and I was fired the next day. Fleury never went to Regina, and the Pats didn't make it to the Memorial Cup.

"Billy liked to drink rum and Coke. That was his trademark. His death shocked me. He was in Palm Springs, I think. Billy had a million-dollar brain."

"Blanchette?"

"Bernie. He always won the scoring race at the Canadiens' training camp — every year. But he couldn't make that team. I don't know why Bernie didn't make it in the NHL. I think there are just guys who don't look like NHL hockey players, so everyone decides they never will be. All Bernie ever did was score goals. I'm not sure what his NHL record was, but I don't remember anyone giving him a good chance. Real nice guy, quiet, worked hard. I don't know where he is today but I'd like to know — Prince Albert, maybe. He's from the West."

"Fonteyne?"

"Beezer! I have no idea why we called him that. He was a mailman from Wetaskiwin. He still lives there. He was 15 years older than me when I played with him, and he'd already had a good NHL career with Detroit, New York, and Pittsburgh. He was the fittest man in hockey. Holy cow, could he skate." With a wink, Jim says, "I bet Beezer could still play today if someone would just give him a shot."

Jim is right — Val Fonteyne is in Wetaskiwin, Alberta, and I'm thrilled to be talking with him. I imagine Val will go down in history as the least penalized player ever, taking only 13 minor penalties in 820 NHL contests, another two in 149 WHA games, and four in 68 total playoff appearances.

"They never talked about my penalty totals when I was playing," Val says. "That was something that came up years after my career was over."

I wonder why this is. I wonder why people of that era didn't take note of Val's puny penalty totals, but today, in a time when players and fans ridicule the Lady Byng trophy — awarded to the NHL's most gentlemanly player — Val's record warrants mention.

Are gentlemen such a rarity these days? Did Val play in an era when sportsmanship was more of an expectation than an exception? "There must have been something about your game that resulted in such stunningly low penalty minutes," I say.

"I did kill a lot of penalties," he replies. "And the last thing you want to do when you're killing a penalty is take another. I was a 'shadow,' often playing against the other teams' top players, trying to keep them from scoring rather than attempting to score myself. When you're trying to keep the top players from scoring, you're not helping your team if you take a penalty doing it."

This too appears to be a part of the game that's changed. Today's

93

attitudes around trash-talking, getting in an opponent's face in an effort to get under his skin, and believing that "if you're not cheating, you're not trying" were clearly not a part of Fonteyne's game.

"I see you were a left-winger — did you shadow Howe?"

With enormous respect for *the man*, Val responds like he's talking about royalty. "Yes. When I was not playing *with* Gordon in Detroit, he was certainly one of the men I was expected to check. But in those days, it didn't matter whether it was left or right wing. You played where you had to play to get the job done. That was my role, checking men like Gordie. But I was only 160 pounds. I wasn't going to throw guys like Gordie around, so I had to skate with them."

But Val doesn't want to talk about himself anymore. "How is Jimmy doing? I haven't seen him since we played together in the early '70s."

I'm happy to bring Val up to date on Jim's status, but I'm too excited about being in the company of a remarkable man to notice I'm controlling the conversation: "Do you remember Jim's 10-point game? I notice you scored a goal and had a couple of assists that night."

"Yes, I remember that game. Jimmy was a big name back then. His game was right up there with Hull and Howe in that league at the time. I remember Al Hamilton played for that team, and Doug Barrie."

"Tell me what you remember about that game, Val. Please?"

"Who were we playing?"

"New York."

"Really? Who was in goal for us?"

"Jack Norris."

"Jack was good. Jacques Plante came along later. I remember Jacques only played home games. I went to the WHA because my wife, Anna, and I were expecting our fourth child, our kids were in school, and the Oilers loaned me a car so I could live at home and drive to games. I remember taking that automobile back to the dealership, and Jacques was there picking up a car. I had played with him in New York with the Rangers. I can't remember exactly why the Canadiens traded him to New York, but it still surprises me to think about how Plante, maybe the all-time greatest, was suddenly playing for fifth or sixth place with guys like me in New York."

"Do you remember who was coaching you the night Jim scored his 10 points?"

"I think Ray Kinasewich was, but I'm not sure because Bill Hunter fired him at some point that year and took over the coaching himself. Then we had Brian Shaw coach us the second year I was there. It was crazy in that league. One night we'd be in Minnesota and the next, Houston. Then we'd go east before returning to Edmonton. I remember playing in New York and we hadn't eaten. Hunter bought us chocolate bars. Imagine that — our pre-game meal at Madison Square Gardens was chocolate bars."

But Val's not done inquiring about Jim. "I read something about Jimmy in the *Edmonton Journal*. I read about his *deal*." I took this to mean Jim's health issues and his battles with the NHL and the Players' Association. "I remember Jimmy's late wife, Liz. She was a very nice girl."

I tell him Jim has landed on his feet in that regard, what with Caroline too being something special.

"Great. That's great news. And it's been great talking to you. When you talk to Jimmy next, tell him I've got a son in Osoyoos. I go down there about once a year. Tell Jimmy, next time I go to see my boy, I'll be dropping in on him. Tell him that, will you, David? Tell him I'll look forward to seeing him."

* * * * * * * * * * * * *

By 1974, because of the competitive presence of the World Hockey Association, professional hockey players were, for the first time, out-earning their baseball and football counterparts, but the WHA's economic environment was never secure. "We always carried our skates with us," Jim says, laughing, "just in case our equipment was seized by the bank. If you had to find new equipment, that was one thing, but if you didn't have your own skates, you couldn't play. Seriously, it was a lot of fun and we all made good money, but you never knew if your next paycheque was going to bounce. That's why I left Cleveland — they bounced cheques on me.

"Most of the players had their money up front, but a lot of guys didn't. In Edmonton I got my contract guaranteed by the bank, but in Cleveland it wasn't part of my deal. That Cleveland team was owned by mafia when I signed, so it was never a question whether they'd make payday. Then they were sold, and before long the new owners went under. They'd built their arena way out in the country and they weren't drawing any fans. We had a bunch of characters on that club, so we had a lot of fun, but the fun stops pretty quick when the cheques start bouncing.

"There was a dispersal draft when they didn't pay us," Jim explains. "I could have gone to Minnesota, but I wasn't sure whether the WHA was still the best fit for me. There were three or four clubs that went bankrupt at the same time, and some other teams were just hanging on by a thread. I remember having to play the New York Raiders in New Jersey when the Raiders couldn't pay the bills in New York. Their equipment had been seized. I had a friend in New York who'd asked to come to the game, so I had some tickets waiting for him and they were those 'Admit One' stubs. Big-league hockey and they're handing out dinky little admission tickets like you'd get at a church raffle. That's when I decided to go back to the NHL.

"Some guys who went to the WHA were in the prime of their careers, and others were on the verge of becoming stars in the NHL. But the NHL owners wouldn't give them the money.

"I was making eleven grand with the Leafs when I first signed with the Oilers for a hundred and twenty thou, plus they gave me a car, all the furniture in my house, and a $75,000 signing bonus. People said to me, 'Oh, they won't be able to come up with the money.' But they did.

"When I played with the Leafs, Liz and I had lawn furniture in our house. I was still borrowing money from my mother. The Leafs didn't care. So the WHA was a big turning point for a lot of careers and for guys to make decent money.

"Bernie Parent had signed on for a big bonus with the Miami Screaming Eagles," Jim recalls. "When he did, everybody ridiculed him. They all said that team wouldn't survive, which turned out to be true, but in the meantime Bernie pocketed a lot of money. So who got the last laugh there?

"Eagleson and Ballard ridiculed the WHA every chance they got. Think about that — here's a new league that's helping to drive up player salaries, and the head of the Players' Association is ridiculing them. Then Ballard, when he heard I was looking to jump, asked that I give him a chance to match any contract. But he'd never have given me anywhere near the money I got. Eagleson said that was why I never got to go back to Toronto — that Harold wasn't happy with me — when I heard elsewhere it was Darryl who didn't want me. Of course, Eagleson was buddies with everyone in Chicago, where I did end up playing.

"But there was no way Ballard was going to give me that big of a raise. Plus I wanted to be close to my fishing lodge in the Northwest Territories, and Edmonton was my hometown in many ways. So I just jumped.

"I admit that now I look back and I would have liked to have had those three or four years in Toronto. And I would like to have had my back looked after by sports people. Some people say a doctor's a doctor, but I didn't find out until years later that the doctors who had operated on me had nicked my nerve — so all those years I suffered with no idea why.

"Like when I was invited to play for Team Canada, it was the biggest thing in the world, but I couldn't even tie my skates up. I ended up playing two or three games, but I could hardly even walk, much less play hockey at that level. I remember having to take some powerful painkillers before I could go on the ice. I was miserable."

It's easy to argue that Canada vs. Russia, as it played out in '72, was everything it has been hailed to be since. And that the men who participated were worthy gladiators. But I find it difficult to get a feel for what Canada vs. Russia 1974 really was.

I'm sure some men on both sides of the Iron Curtain had seen how much money could be made from such a tournament, and the WHA was looking for further exposure. I suspect the Russians wanted to redeem themselves against an inferior opponent. I imagine that some Canadian men, especially those who didn't qualify to play in '72, welcomed the chance to ply their skills against the Soviet Union's best — while Canadian fans hoped their boys might once again be able to capture lightning in a bottle.

But Team Canada '74 didn't stand a chance of acquiring a legacy to rival that of their predecessors, despite great efforts from their warriors. One of whom was Jim. Having played some excellent hockey in Edmonton the previous season, Jim should have been a sure bet to represent his country. But this was not so. His back injuries plagued him throughout the summer, and he showed up out of shape and in considerable discomfort. His critics said he wouldn't be able to skate with the Russians on their large ice surface and that his aggressive style of play would result in penalties against the unflappable Russian juggernaut.

His critics proved correct. Jim played in only three games in the eight-game tournament, recording two assists and three penalties — a slashing major, one minor for cross-checking, and another for charging. When I broach the subject, Jim clearly doesn't want to discuss it: "Yeah, well, my back hurt and I was out of shape. What can I say? I ran over [Vladislav] Tretiak one game. How's that?"

Shortly after the series ended, the Oilers traded Jim to the Cleveland Crusaders, where he played two more injury-shortened seasons — one in which he performed well and the other really well.

But other than the quiet success he was having in that Ohio hockey outpost, what was it about a late-20s Jim that compelled a 17-year-old man-child like me to continue to follow his career so closely? I suppose our history together was a factor, that there was still enough 12-year-old in me that I wasn't ready to let him go.

But by 1976, both our lives had changed dramatically. Jim, with a young family, was playing in an unconventional market, nursing serious injuries both chronic and acute. I was running with a wolf pack all my own, entering the work world full-time for the first time. My hormones, clearly the boss of me, were attempting to make hockey an afterthought. It would have been easy for me to drift away from the things that had mattered to me as a child. Yet that didn't happen. The game, and Jim, still had a grip on me, even though the business that is professional hockey had begun to turn me off.

But while I could see the part that Jim's jumping to the WHA had played in helping other players of that era acquire satisfactory salaries, at the time I didn't understand the perilous gamble he and other stars had taken. Leaving for the WHA meant risking retribution — being ignored or blackballed — by the NHL and the men who managed it, for the association's significant role in escalating wages. And playing in the rival league meant chancing injury for organizations that might not last.

What I couldn't comprehend as a kid was how the courage of these men in taking on this risk would play such a large role in setting up huge financial rewards for future players. The WHA and the rebels who braved it were clearly the catalysts for today's enormous NHL salaries, making those who led the way working-class heroes. So, somehow, I intuitively knew that whatever else might be catching my adolescent attention, Jim Harrison remained well worth watching.

* * * * * * * * * * * * *

When Jim's hockey career came to a close with the NHL's Chicago Black Hawks, I wasn't paying attention. I'd suffered a huge loss earlier that year when my 26-year-old sister and her husband died in a car crash at Clappison's Corners, in Ontario. A transport truck driver, heading north, fell asleep behind the wheel and crossed what in 1979 was a white center line.

My sister and brother-in-law, travelling south, didn't stand a chance. I was at the family home in Kitchener when a good friend waiting for them in Hamilton called to say that my sister and her hubby hadn't arrived. Given their responsible nature, enough time had elapsed since they had left their house that any hope their absence could be explained in a non-threatening way was no longer possible.

I called the police, and after a series of questions from them to clarify who I was and where we were, they simply said they would be at our home shortly. While I moved as quickly as I could toward denial, my parents knew better — Wendy and Robert were dead. I'll never forget watching my mom in all her sadness and rage try to impart a physical beating on one of those big cops. She was obviously feeling pain that I, a childless male, will never be able to comprehend or describe with mere words.

Dad responded by going on an angry, 10-year alcoholic binge, making life miserable for my mother and little brother, who was only eight when the tragedy began. The rest of us, all young adults by then, bailed. To this day, I can't imagine what life looked like to my mom, who, at 49, suddenly had a young child, a drunk, and a dead daughter and son-in-law to deal with for a decade. While not the same circumstance as Jim's loss of Liz less than two decades later, my family found itself in a comparable crisis at a similar stage of life. So my last memories of Jim's playing days are foggy. I don't remember the tryout Glen Sather gave him with one of the NHL's newest entries in Edmonton, after the NHL absorbed the Oilers and three other WHA teams, a merger that rendered the rebel league dead.

"I too don't look back at that time fondly," Jim says with a sigh. "Not only was my back not up for that Edmonton opportunity, but things hadn't ended well in Chicago. Chicago was where the team doctor lied to me. That's why now every player goes to his own doctor. Of course they do. Who the heck do you think is paying the team doctor? So now there are all these players with all this money — why wouldn't they get another opinion?

"I had this sharp pain in my back that ran from my butt to my heel. So the Black Hawks team doctor injects something into me that he tells me will dissolve the parts of the disk in my back that are causing me so much pain. He calls the procedure an epidural block. But it turns out he didn't give me an epidural block. He gave me a placebo — a shot of sugar — to see if I'm faking. It's all right there in my medical records," Jim says, pointing to a big box between us. "What did I do, dream up those operations? Put those scars on my back myself?"

Jim eases away from me for a moment. He's far from done, so I suspect he is trying to collect some unresolved anger. "The next year, Rangers Dean Talafous cross-checks me and my leg goes numb," he finally continues. "I tell the team doctor this. And I tell him that my coach, Bob Pulford — a former teammate of mine in Toronto — won't give me any time to rest. Then the doctor tells Pulford what I said — that he's a slave driver — and things with Pulford and me got really bad after that.

"Three days later I can't move, so I take some Valium and climb into the whirlpool. Pulford comes along and asks me to play. I was the team's tough guy, he tells me, and they needed me. I told him, 'I can't even walk,' and he says, 'There's nothing wrong with you.' He tells me to 'Go rot in hell' and then sends me to Moncton, where the Hawks' farm team was. Pulford pissed on more players . . . Chicago is famous for that.

"I refused to go to Moncton, so Pulford suspends me without pay. Then I give Eagleson a call; he'd been my agent for six years. I figured we'd file a grievance. But Eagleson sends me to an old buddy of his, Dr. Bull, for a second opinion. Dr. Bull determined my most recent back operation resulted in nerve damage and that Talafous' cross-check made it worse. Then, because I'm feeling like someone's stuck a knife in me, Dr. Bull gives me some painkiller and tells me to rest. But I'm still not getting paid, so *finally* we file a grievance.

"Things got really complicated after that because my agent, Eagleson, was also Pulford's agent. The two of them had been friends since childhood. Plus, Pulford was an employee of Hawks owner Bill Wirtz, and Wirtz and Eagleson were best buddies. Then John Ziegler was assigned to judge my grievance. Ziegler? He was the NHL president — that means Wirtz paid part of his salary. Got that? The guy reviewing my grievance was an employee of the organization I'd filed my grievance against. And the guy I'm paying to look out for me in all this was best buddies with the guys I'd officially complained about. He was even getting paid to act on behalf of one of them.

"By this point, Liz is livid. She's driving me everywhere — I've got spasms so bad I've got to lie down in the back of our station wagon — and she can't believe they can't see how bad I'm hurting."

Jim is full of emotion, moving around the room. I'm not sure if his actions are rooted in his love for Liz or his dislike for some of the other individuals he's commenting on. "We were all told to go to a meeting — me, Liz, Eagleson, Pulford, Bobby [Orr, whose playing days were over and who was working as an assistant to Pulford], Dr. Kolb [Chicago's team doctor], and Hawks trainer Skip Thayer. Keith Magnuson was supposed to be there. He was one of my teammates. He used to drive me to the rink, so I asked him to speak about how he had to lift my legs out of the car some days because I couldn't do it myself, but he couldn't make it to the meeting. The next year Chicago named him head coach. Suspicious, don't you think?

"We were going into the room, and Eagleson told me Dr. Kolb and the trainers were against me, that he'd take care of everything, but that I wasn't supposed to speak. Then Pulford said, 'We're sending him to Moncton. There's nothing wrong with him.' And Eagleson doesn't ask any questions or tell them anything from our point of view. So I said, 'I can't believe what you guys are saying.' Eagleson turns to me and yells, 'I told you to shut up!' Right in front of everybody. By this point I'm crying, I'm so angry. I yelled, 'I can't believe this! I can't walk! And you guys think I'm faking!'

"After listening to what we all had to say, Ziegler tells everyone to leave the room except for Eagleson, Pulford, and Bobby, so they can make a ruling on my grievance. Half an hour later, Eagleson comes out and tells me I have to go to the minors. He just said, 'That's the rules if you want to get paid.' So I went to the minors. What was I going to do? I had three kids to feed and bills to pay.

"Then," says Jim, "I find out Ziegler didn't really say I had to go to the minors. What he'd actually done was tell the Hawks that they hadn't followed proper procedure. There are things you've got to do before you send a player down, and they hadn't done them. As a result, all Ziegler was allowed to do was look at my grievance as a discussion. He couldn't make a ruling on it. Sending me to the minors was something Eagleson and Pulford cooked up. Bobby confirmed it years later."

Now it's me that's speechless. Did I hear that right — "Sending me to the minors was something Eagleson and Pulford cooked up"? But Jim's got no time for my dumbfounded feelings — he is already recalling an ill-fated trip east. "So now I'm in the minors, in Moncton, New Brunswick. And things really begin to come off the tracks for me — that's when I started mixing alcohol and pills. But it's also in Moncton where I first convinced myself that my playing days were over. So I applied for disability insurance, and the insurance company told me to go to the Mayo Clinic in Minnesota. They wanted me to get a few more medical opinions, which was fine except the Hawks wouldn't send them my medical records.

"The doctors in Minnesota said I'd need another operation. But no one would pay for it. No one would even pay the bills I was running up at the clinic. I had to pay ten grand out of my own pocket to cover expenses. You can hardly go ahead with an operation in the U.S. on those terms.

"So I asked Eagleson to draw up my retirement papers," Jim explains. "He wrote that I wouldn't be going after anyone with any lawsuits or medical claims. I was sitting in his office when I read this, and I told him I wouldn't sign a letter like that, and he said, 'You fucking hockey players think you're something. Go get another lawyer.' So that's what I did. I went and got another lawyer. But when Al found out, he threatened to throw my files on Bay Street if I didn't get in right away to pick them up. So I went in and got them, and most of my things weren't even in the box — including the letter we'd written asking for disability insurance.

"Then Eagleson told me that I couldn't apply for Workers' Compensation in Illinois, which was bullshit. After I did finally apply, I'd go to meetings and Wirtz's lawyers wouldn't show. I'd fly to Buffalo and when I got there, I'd wait around until someone told me that Wirtz's lawyers had cancelled the meeting. The whole thing dragged on so long that Workers' Comp eventually ruled I'd taken too long to apply so I no longer qualified.

"In the end, I got less than 10 percent of the $120,000 disability insurance I was entitled to. I could have fought harder but I needed the money and couldn't tie it up in the system any longer."

Jim, standing only two feet from me, looks me straight in the eyes. "That was just the beginning of my education — that was when I started to see what was going on between the league and Eagleson. That's when guys began to wonder why Al wouldn't allow for salary disclosure. He even told the guys who were playing at the time not to talk to the old-timers. But because Eagleson determined his own salary, he gave himself a $50,000-a-year pension when some of the game's greatest stars were getting less than ten grand.

"Everyone was too afraid of Eagleson to say anything because Al could make you look stupid. And everyone knew that Al could hurt your chances at a job after you retired if you crossed him. Just look at Pulford, Bobby Clarke, Tony Esposito, Dale Tallon . . . If you were one of Eagleson's buddies, like those guys are, there was always a job for you somewhere, but if you crossed him . . . Heck, I've got letters in this box that have both the NHL and the Players' Association on the same letterhead. What do you think was going on there?

"Then Jean Beliveau wanted to know why the Players' Association wasn't looking after the old guys who were having tough times —

guys like Doug Harvey. And Brad Park asked where all the money from the Canada Cup went.

"Beliveau, Park, and then guys like Carl Brewer and a few others were really smart and way ahead of their time. They started to figure out that players were getting screwed by our own Players' Association long before the rest of us schmucks did.

"All these chicken-shit newspaper reporters used to say, 'I'll check into it,' but none of them did, until Russ Conway. It took an American like Conway to investigate because all the Canadian newspaper guys had their heads up Eagleson's ass. Al was so tight with the Conservative Party, he could just phone up some [Conservative] newspaper and say, 'I don't want your guy covering hockey anymore,' and poof! Your job would be gone.

"Eagleson had control over all hockey jobs. Even the greatest hockey player who ever lived — Bobby Orr — lost his job with the Bruins because Al wanted him elsewhere. Bobby never wanted to leave Boston. But Al, who did all Bobby's negotiating, told him the Bruins didn't want him, so that's how Bobby ended up in Chicago. But the Bruins *did* want him — enough that they'd offered him part-ownership of the hockey club. But Eagleson wanted Bobby to sign with his buddies in Chicago so he didn't tell him about the Bruins' ownership offer.

"Other guys were filing for insurance — insurance they were perfectly entitled to — and Eagleson was charging them large lawyers' fees for going after it. 'They're going to give us a hard time,' he'd say. 'I'll have to put some good lawyers on it.' And then the player would get a big bill from Eagleson's lawyers. But there never were any lawyers. The player had already, easily, qualified for the insurance that they'd been paying into. The 'hard time' Eagleson said they were going to get was all make-believe. Everything was make-believe except Al's invoice."

Not exactly inclined to living in the past, despite how it seems some days, the practical Jim directs his diatribe back to today.

"Even now, the Players' Association doesn't return my calls. But NHL commissioner Gary Bettman calls me back right away. What's wrong with that picture? The commissioner's office treats me better than my Players' Association does? It's because of NHL vice-president Brian O'Neill that I own anything at all. Brian and the NHL paid the second mortgage on my house when I couldn't.

"All the players and newspaper guys used to say to me, 'Eagleson's powerful; you're a nut to take him on.' But that's just the way I am. That's the way I react when something happens that I think might be wrong or unfair — I fight.

"Even now, I'm not convinced that Eagleson didn't send you here to mess with me. How do I know he didn't hire you to come here pretending to be a writer and saying I was your favourite player when you were a kid? So that you could make my life miserable because of some of the things I've said about him. Huh? How do I know what you're actually going to write? How do I know I'm not going to have to fight with you?"

* * * * * * * * * * * * * *

"Eventually," Jim says, "everybody who was supposed to be looking after me — the NHL, the Players' Association, Eagleson, the Black Hawks, and all their doctors — said, 'Well, we did everything for Harrison that we possibly can.' Bullshit you did. I'm not that stupid. Then I find out later, when Carl Brewer takes me to a doctor that he trusted, that my nerve is entrapped in scar tissue.

"So all this stuff that Chicago had me doing — all their therapy, standing on my head, stretching my back backwards — it was all just making things worse, because I had this entrapped nerve. That's why it felt like they were hitting me with a hammer.

"Until Carl's doctor said, 'We can try to fix this, but the chances are if we do, the scar tissue will come back just as good, or worse.' He told me he thought I had to learn to live with it. 'You have to lose some weight,' he said. I've always been heavy, because if I'm in pain I'll sit at the dinner table and eat two steaks.

"Then I went to the National Academy of Sports Medicine in Phoenix and they said, 'We can correct some of this.' They figured out that just walking was irritating my entrapped nerve. So I started working with them. Within three months I started feeling better. I stopped taking Tylenol pills and now, I'm not pain-free — not even close — but I'll tell you, it's made a million dollars' worth of difference. Six years ago, I'd sit around and drink 26 ounces of whisky and mix it with painkillers, giving me gut rot, but today I can get around a little.

"But why should it have taken so long to have it looked after? If I would have known right from the beginning what was wrong, not have to go through all those medical records to find out for myself, all those CAT scans and everything else. Just to find out that the doctor had nicked my nerve when he was operating on me, and that the resulting scar tissue was entrapping that nerve . . .

"That really is my problem — the entrapment caused by scar tissue, and how my body compensates for it, weakens me. That's what they do these days. You tell them your shoulder hurts and they go to work on treating your whole body, not just your shoulder — unless you get a major injury to your shoulder, of course. Otherwise, they look at all the connections.

"Because now, after they evaluate me, they'll come back and say, 'I think it's your knee that's increasing that pain in your back,' and I'll say, 'Oh yeah, I do have a bad knee.' Then they'll say, 'To help you with your back, we've got to straighten that knee out.' It makes sense to me. If I can't walk straight, I'm putting pressure on my back, right?"

Suddenly aware of his posture, Jim stands up straighter than usual. "I'm no expert, but I'm learning. I'm just saying this is what has worked best for *me*. If it weren't for Carl Brewer's doctor in Calgary and the National Academy of Sports Medicine in Phoenix,

I'd be in a real mess. But I've had to pay for way too much of this out of my own pocket. The Players' Association won't have anything to do with helping me with costs.

"I had my first back operation when I was 18. Carl's doctor said that probably I had a lot of back pain and scar tissue then, but I was likely strong enough and in good enough shape to compensate for it. I didn't have too many problems in those days except for broken wrists and noses — nothing that affected my back. I worked hard, and my posture was probably better than it is today.

"I likely had scar tissue that eventually got so bad I couldn't take it anymore. It's no wonder I had pain 24 hours a day after they operated and nicked the nerve."

After 40 seconds of improved posture, Jim leans forward again to point at his foot. "Right now, I have no feeling in my big right toe. You could drop a rock on that toe and I'd have no idea you did it, because that nerve is dead. I don't even think about it anymore. I just live with it. Same with the arthritis that accompanies it — from my back to my big toe. A lot of times I'll fall. Maybe I'll come across a hole or something — you know when you are supposed to feel something in your foot that tells you there is a hole there? I don't have that. Suddenly I'll go down. Boom! It'll be because I have no feeling in that leg. It all starts at that toe. I ask myself: Should I have more surgery? Will I get scar tissue again? What do I do 'til they can come up with some new technology?

"The best thing for me is to learn how to live with it. That was the best advice I could ever have got from Carl's doctor — Dr. Baker. He said there are things they can do with surgery, but it'll all still result in scar tissue welding to scar tissue. I was told they literally had to take a chisel to it in my last operation. No wonder they nicked that nerve."

Jim sighs. "You don't think about it when you're playing. I didn't. I wouldn't even be able to have a conversation like this because I wouldn't know how to, and I didn't care. I just knew I wanted to play tomorrow. Now I listen to what the doctor has to say. But I could never have gone to the Chicago Black Hawks and said I'm not playing. When I did say to them that I was disabled, they said, 'Bullshit.' So what was I to do? I kept playing. I wanted to get paid. I had three young kids, and I'd just finally made some money. So you fool them. Even now my whole leg is hurting, but I've just got to work it out.

"It was only after I connected with Carl's doctor, the National Academy of Sports Medicine, and NHL vice-president Brian O'Neill, who gave me emergency funding so I could travel to Phoenix for medical help, that, for the first time in years, things were actually beginning to look up.

"Who'd have ever thought when I was playing that a private company would end up giving me better medical care than some of the so-called best sports doctors in the world? And that the NHL Players' Association — my union — would tell me to go to hell?"

* * * * * * * * * * * * * * *

While out walking one of Kelowna's lovely nature trails, Jim and I stumble upon a dozen baby quails. Scrambling for safety while their mother quietly signals to them from a nearby escape route, they look like raindrops as they move across the leafy groundcover. Jim could hold all 12 of them in one of his meaty palms, and the way he eases himself down onto his bare knees to get close to them, I think he might try.

Seeing a man with such a serious hunting history and a reputation for brawling melt at the sight of those babies has me once again considering the complexity of the human condition. How, on one hand, Jim will laugh and joke as he tells you how it felt to have his hands around Terry Harper's throat. How he was looking out of the corner of his eye for tough-guy Ted Harris who

he intuitively knew was "looking for his chance to join the dance."
Yet Jim grows giddy when he sees those baby birds. And then sad
when he speaks about the risks related to fighting.

"Once upon a time I supported fighting," he says. "But today
I'm a father and a grandfather, right? Hearing about young Don
Sanderson dying while playing senior hockey in Whitby doesn't
sit well with me. It's simply not necessary that someone die in a
hockey fight. It makes no sense.

"People are afraid to admit it, but if you look at some of the
fighters today and the whole depression thing that so many of
them are dealing with, I think a lot of it is prescription drugs and
steroids. They don't call them steroids anymore — they've got
different names for them and they mask them — but what those
guys are taking isn't good for them.

"Everybody has personal trainers, they all work out in gyms for
12 months of the year, and I can tell you I know athletes — young
kids — taking steroids. In my era it was alcohol. Today it's drugs.

"When you look at the problems some of the old players have
with alcohol, you can see where it started, because that was our way
of life. Today's kids, they all want to be something that they're not,
and a lot of that means bulking up. So I really think the suicides
you're seeing have something to do with drugs. I don't have any
basic research on it, but I don't need any when all I want to do is
keep kids safe. I've talked to some doctors, and they'll tell you that
what we called steroids, the kids are taking them and the results are
just terrible. I know parents with young kids that are committing
suicide, and a lot of it is their lifestyle. If you've seen some of the
before-and-after pictures, you don't have to be a genius to know
what's going on.

"I've seen people take steroids," Jim recalls. "My last few years
in the NHL I saw guys smoking marijuana, which was unheard of,
so what else do you think they might have been doing? And what
do you think these kids are doing now, more than 30 years later?

"Like it or not, we were role models, and some days we weren't very good at it. But in my era, being an athlete was a whole different thing. We didn't have TV or newspaper guys following us around, and when we did something wrong it was covered up quickly. One summer I got in a big brawl in a bar in Kamloops when I was playing for the Leafs — the police got involved and I got sued for kicking a guy in the face. But *you* never heard about it, did you? Today it would be all over the internet."

He's right. "It's tougher to be that athlete now. You've got to be squeaky clean. There are lots of guys around like that, but there are others that are making big mistakes. Some of them are obviously struggling with all the attention, while others are stressed with the choices available to them.

"I remember needing 45 stitches to close a wound around my eye, in 1969. We were killing a penalty against the Dallas Black Hawks and I went to block a shot from Jimmy Stanfield — Freddie's brother. Jimmy had a big curve and he was Dallas' top shooter. They were a pretty good hockey team. I took Jimmy's shot right in the eye. In the hospital they thought I was going to lose that eye.

"I remember lying in bed, many times, crying that my hockey career was over. I really figured I would never play again. Pretty close call, I'd say. My point is that while I'm lying there crying, if someone had told me they could restore my vision so I could return to playing hockey, and that all I needed to do was take some magic pill or stick another needle in me, I'd have taken that pill *and* that needle, no questions asked. That's why you need somebody else looking out for you — somebody like your Players' Association."

With all the genuineness a man can muster, Jim says, "I would love for the Players' Association to take me to court — I'd get myself heard. I've told them, 'You guys are no better than when Eagleson was there.' I've asked them, 'Are you sure Eagleson isn't still running things behind the scenes?' It doesn't matter how many times they change the guys in charge, none of them have ever cared about the old players and the problems those guys are having. I'm not just talking about the things *I* need. We have old-time players on skid row and on welfare that the Players' Association will not help.

"Yet they've got money for players to go to the Arctic, golfing, drinking, everybody having a great time. Meanwhile, we've got guys dying after partying at golf tournaments, and others have gone to jail for what happened when they tried to drive home.

"I admit I'm still stuck in the old days in many ways, but I'm no longer carrying on like it's 1973. They might not invite Eagleson to their parties anymore, but these Players' Association guys are still an old boys' club, and they still criticize the guys who stand up to them. It's like it's against the law to have a different opinion than they do.

"And it's like they think I should be ashamed of the things I'm fighting for. Not a chance. I'm proud that I was a hockey player. I worked hard to get where I did. The guys would say, 'We're certainly not playing this game for the money.' We all knew we had the best job in the world, but too few of us knew anything about business.

"And when I was fighting, it was never premeditated," Jim adds. "I guarantee you that. Not like these poor guys today, where all of their fights are choreographed coaching decisions. I look at their size, power, physical conditioning, and the steroids some of them have to be taking. I see the lack of respect they have for each other, and I'm honestly scared for their safety. In my day, we fought because either we were pissed off at someone or they were pissed off at us.

"I never thought twice when I was a kid, or later when I was playing, about whether fighting was good or bad. I don't know anyone who did. But the world has changed. Fighting is no longer acceptable in life. Maybe fighting should no longer be acceptable in hockey.

"I still watch hockey all the time, and I never turn it on thinking I want to see a fight. I couldn't care less. Some of the best games

I've ever seen — playoff games — I don't ever think about there being no fights in those games. But the NHL doesn't want fighting out of the game. I saw a bunch of the Leafs fight on TV last night. It was premeditated bullshit.

"That stuff about 'Who is the toughest?' That's not real either. Never, when I played, was someone trying to make himself out to be 'The Toughest.' We just didn't think that way. Every guy I fought was tough. Vic Hadfield might not have been considered a fighter, but I didn't want him landing one on *my* nose.

"I know if some magazine put together a list of the toughest guys," Jim says, "they'd name Philadelphia's Dave Schultz from his Broad Street Bully days. But Schultz wasn't tough. He was this skinny kid who suddenly built himself up. He got real big, real fast. Then he became a gang fighter. You seldom saw him square off against one guy. He'd wait until the whole bunch of them were fighting and someone had hold of another guy, and then he'd start whaling away at that first guy he saw who had his arms tied up. If Schultz hadn't played on the Flyers when they were gang fighters, you'd never have heard of him.

"Bob Kelly — now there was the tough guy on that team. Schultz tried to come across as crazy, but Bob didn't have to. Bob was *really* tough. Some people confuse 'crazy' with 'tough.' But there's a difference. Guys would say, 'Harrison's crazy.' I don't think I was crazy. Like I've said, it goes way back for me. I'd be 16 years old and working in a sawmill, and some guy would tell me to do some dirty job that *he* didn't want to do. I didn't think, 'I'm just a kid, I can't stand up to this adult' — I'd just tell him to go to hell, that I wasn't going to do his dirty work and no one was going to make me.

"My brother taught me when I was little that if I didn't stand up for myself I was going to get pushed around. Did fighting help me get into hockey? Yeah. Guys like Scotty Munroe and Ernie MacLean figured out that if I saw someone getting pushed around I'd jump in. So they went to work on helping me develop other hockey skills. When Scotty and Ernie figured out I wasn't going to school anymore, they made me do skating drills every morning.

"It wasn't very often someone dropped their gloves before me, but it was still just a reaction. They'd done something that made me want to fight them. I still react, and I still fight, just not with my fists anymore. I see things all the time — could be the cops, the guys who run hockey, politicians . . . When I see them do something that's not right, it might not make any difference to me, but I'll see it's not good for somebody, so I say something. I start swinging in a different kind of way."

He shrugs his shoulders. "Maybe I should give up the kind of fighting I do now. It's obvious it's no better for me than fist fighting. It's not good for my health or my marriage. Or maybe I have to find a different way to do it.

"When I played, the *way* we fought was different. You might see some old films of guys squaring off, but it was usually just a punch or two. That's why I liked playing when John D'Amico was a linesman. He'd tell me, 'When I jump in to break up a fight you're in, I'll always grab the other guy first — by his arm. That means you've got a chance to get one last punch in before we separate the two of you.' In some fights, that was the only punch I landed.

"We all knew who the cheap-shot artists were — like the slew footers. Nobody respected those guys. But it was the job of a lot of us to police guys like that, not just one or two guys on every team doing all the dirty work. That was the honour in the game that's not there today.

"Now they teach fighting. Like, if you're fighting a right-hander, you want to keep moving to your right, so the guy you're fighting with can't land a good one because you're always pulling a little bit away from him. Fighters work harder to tie a guy's punching hand up today." Jim laughs and then grimaces while he twists his torso, his fists clenched in an effort to show me what he's trying to say. "In my day, I'd just close my eyes and swing away.

"I remember the first time I paired up with Tiger Williams. He grabbed me by the wrist and gave it a little twist, and I thought, 'Whoa, what's going on here?' Tiger was that strong, and he had the technique down before the rest of us did. He had a real edge to him. You had to be careful around him because he was really sneaky. He'd say, 'How are you?' but you knew he'd hit a friend. He and his wife were really good to us when Liz was sick in Vancouver. They gave us a car to use. He's a great guy, but when you played against him, you had to be on guard."

I tell Jim that, many years ago, I drove down to the Six Nations Native community near Brantford, Ontario, looking for former Bruin Stan Jonathan. I went on the premise that I was after Jonathan's autograph, but to be honest I hadn't really hunted autographs for years.

What is an autograph? It's proof of purchase that you've had a brush with fame. Selfies are the same. As an adult, I don't understand why I need to prove that I've spent time with someone whose work I value. I've either shared a couple of words with him and shook his hand or I haven't. But going in search of Jonathan's signature that day was the excuse I needed to connect with the best fighter I've ever seen.

Jim weighs in. "Jonathan was one of the toughest punchers ever. Stan was in the category of a John Ferguson. That was the thing with Fergy — I wouldn't fight with a veteran like him. He didn't have to put up with me. He had a job to do, scoring 20 goals a year. I was expected to respect that.

"Garry Howatt was tough too. They used to say when Howatt fought that you'd have to kill him before he'd stop. Good for Garry.

"Larry Robinson, another tough guy. Not that he fought that often — he didn't have to.

"Henri Richard was tough too — *really* tough. I fought him a few times. Even when he was older, he was scary tough like a bantam rooster. I bet fans don't remember him that way. And I remember fighting Dick Duff. I guess I was trying to prove myself or I'd taken a run at him or done something stupid. He was a great player so he shouldn't have had to fight a young jerk like me. But he did. I have a lot of respect for Dick. He was a little guy and a great scorer, but he never backed down from anybody. You learned quickly with Dick not to mess with him.

"Wayne Cashman — another lefty you'd have to watch out for. No one wanted to fight Cash, but every playoff he'd have to take care of one or two guys on the other team.

"You want to talk about tough guys? Paul Shmyr. Skinny guy, you'd never know to look at him what a fighter he was. But he was captain on every team he ever played on.

"You know who was really tough? The toughest I ever met? Eddie Johnston, that's who — a goalie! But goalies don't have to fight. So I'm telling you that you could just feel Eddie's toughness when you were around him. Eddie's toughness was real. Eddie's toughness was something everybody who knew him respected."

I think I get it and want to tell Jim so. But best not to interrupt him right now; he's talking about a subject he deserves an honorary doctorate for.

"So this debate about 'Who's the toughest?' is a waste of time. All those guys I named were tough, and there were lots of others like them.

"I watched Bob Probert — he could play some hockey and he was tough. But these modern guys that can only fight and can't play hockey? It's not their fault. They're just boys who want to play in the NHL and you can't blame them for that. But they're just puppets for their coaches. And if the NHL and the Players' Association don't soon find a new way to define 'tough,' one of those young boys is going to die in a hockey fight. How'd you like to be their parents or grandparents?"

* * * * * * * * * * * * * * * *

Given the shortness of a professional athlete's career, it is likely his playing days will be over before his children can appreciate — or possibly even remember — his privileged work. Not so with Jim's oldest son, Justin, who was born in Scarborough, Ontario, in 1971, when Jim was barely 24.

"I remember skating at old Chicago Stadium when my dad played for the Black Hawks," Justin recalls. "There were those big stairs there, when it was time to go on and off the ice. My dad would tell me, 'Go skate the circles,' so off I'd go. Guys would say I skated like my dad, and my dad would say, 'That's not a good thing,' and everybody would laugh.

"I'd skate with the team most Saturday mornings. It was an optional practice for the players — it was a game day. So my dad would go for a light skate and then spend the rest of his time with me. I remember once I got to take 10 shots on Tony Esposito; the story is I scored on five of them."

Justin and I are talking on the telephone, me from the southwest coast of Newfoundland and him on the top end of Vancouver Island, where he flies float planes. The day is winding down where I am, but Justin probably has things to do.

"Yeah, but I'm only too glad to talk about my dad, so I've got lots of time for you," he says. "I never miss a chance to tell anyone my dad played professional hockey. I'm proud of him — *real* proud.

"Oh, I might have taken a little crap from other kids around Minor Atom age. There was always the comparison thing going on, and some kids would say, 'You're only on the team because your father is an NHL hockey player,' but that was kid stuff. Their parents all wanted to meet my dad.

"I've never played any high-end hockey myself, but wherever I do play, I never miss a chance to tell the guys my dad played pro — especially in Canada, eh?

"I have memories from as far back as two and a half, flying in the float plane we'd be taking to my dad's camp. Orr and Sittler would be there. My dad was a pretty lucky guy — not because he played in the NHL, but because my mom was one open-hearted woman."

It's raining in Chandler, Arizona. The temperature is in the mid-'60s. "A nice break from the sun," Jim's youngest son, Trevor, says. Trevor is a sports-injury consultant, with a client list that includes basketball icon Shaquille O'Neal. I've talked to a lot of people about Jim, none any more helpful than Trevor. He wants to assist with whatever is important to his father.

"My dad didn't talk with us kids about all that stuff that went on with Alan Eagleson. So when I read about what happened to him, in Russ Conway's *Game Misconduct*, I was in tears. I don't know if I could read that book again."

I ask Trevor when he first remembers noticing his dad's occupation was different than that of other fathers.

"Middle school," he says, "when he and my mom moved the family to Estevan so Dad could coach there. Estevan was such a small town, I figured out that I couldn't get away with anything because everyone knew who my dad was, and he'd eventually find out. Otherwise, outside of hockey, he didn't really lead a life a whole lot different than anyone else. I'd say I had a pretty typical upbringing.

"My best childhood memory is of the trips we took to the Northwest Territories. We'd take a whole month and go up to our camp. It was such a great time, and to spend it almost entirely with my dad was special.

"But I never realized the pain he was in — and not just him, all those guys who played the game, so many of them still hurting, 24 hours a day, seven days a week. My dad might not talk about it with family very much, but you can see it in the way he walks. Mario Lemieux was my favourite player when I was a kid, but today my heroes are my dad and my sister. Have you talked to Ardin? Do you need her number?"

Mother of four, wife, corporate entrepreneur, health advocate, track coach, grad student (exercise science), triathlete . . . Ardin Tucker does it all. And to top it off, she's beautiful. So, when I catch up with Jim's only daughter at her home in Atlanta, Georgia, I really don't need to ask her why her sibling lists her as one of his heroes. But I hope she might be able to give me something I haven't already learned from her brother bragging about her.

"Well, Trevor and I are closest in age," she begins. "We've just always been there for each other, and I guess because he was younger than me I took care of him in a lot of ways, like after our mom took sick. He's been there for me too. I had my first child as a freshman at college. I was a single mom for many years. So without the support of family . . .

"That's what it's all about isn't it — family? I know that's cliché and a lot of people, when they hear the word *family*, picture everybody sitting down over the holidays and enjoying a meal, but family to me is about going through challenges together. Nobody left behind or on their own. That's how *I* think it should be.

"It's what you do when you're confronted with challenges, because everybody has challenges — that's just life. But family can face those challenges together. And that's something I learned from my parents. I learned so much from them. Just look at my dad and what he's done to confront *his* challenges.

"Same when my oldest son had his problems with partial paralysis; my dad just dug in and did what had to be done to support Nate. They've got an incredible bond, those two do — Dad and Nate. I wish you could see it. It's magical. Not that my dad's relationship with his other grandkids isn't wonderful, but it's like my dad is Nate's angel, and my dad's strength has helped Nate through."

A dozen years younger than her husband, Caroline Cheney Harrison is eye-catching, curvy, and fit — and I've got her alone. Meaning any man with an ounce of double entendre in his soul has to smile when she says, "I don't believe I have anything that could be of any use to you, David." Of course, my cheap thrill comes only because Caroline's been denied a fair chance to complete her comment: ". . . because I wasn't around in Jim's hockey-playing days."

But even without such self-indulgent innuendo, I find Caroline's comment comical. Caroline is a strong, clever, articulate individual who has more carefully considered opinions to share than most people. And, while she cautiously pauses to ponder a little longer than her hubby does before answering inquiries, she withholds nothing.

So I ask her how she deals with Jim's anger — rage that results from a toxic blend of chronic back pain and a belief that many hockey men care about little more than what is within their wallets.

"Two ways," she tells me. "I deal with Jim's temper two ways. One, it hurts me to see how Jim's hurts hurt him, so at times I attempt to say things that I'm hoping will help him to see things differently.

"And the second way is, when I piece things together for myself, I see he is right. He is owed something; he does live in pain. So while Jim and I are quite different in the way we handle things — he's passionate, while I'm more of an optimist — I do see he's right in what he's fighting for, so I try to support him. I just don't want his anger to suck away his remaining years.

"Jim would not be happy if he knew I was telling you about his physical pain," Caroline adds. "But he leans all the time, because his back hurts so badly. There are days I need to help him get out of bed. I think that sometimes it's only his God-given gifts — he's got good genes — that allow him to manage as well as he does.

"Something I wish you could see are those rare occasions where Jim tries something physical. Oh. Oh-oh, here we go again. If someone from Disability hears me talk about when Jim does something physical . . ." Caroline, stressed at the thought that suspicious insurance authorities might suggest Jim, because he occasionally attempts something of a bodily nature, must not honestly be experiencing pain, collects herself before carrying on. "But it doesn't matter if it is floor hockey, ping-pong, or pickle-ball, Jim's got this natural athletic ability and an incredible, ultra-competitive spirit. He's amazing — I'm in awe of his ability.

"But he also makes me mad because I'd like to win once in a while. Once, we had been into some wine and I thought maybe I could beat him at ping-pong. He pulverized me. Then I found out he was playing with his left hand."

Caroline shifts in her seat. She doesn't want to talk about fun and games anymore. "You know, David, when I took up with Jim, shortly after Liz's death, some people thought I was the devil. I still fudge the timing when people ask how long Jim and I have been together, so they don't get the idea that things were going on with us before Liz's death."

Caroline laughs a nervous laugh when she tells me she believes it is "odd" that I call on her to tell part of the story of Jim's late wife. She rightly notes that the current wife's take on the former wife's story is not the usual path to an accurate, unbiased account. But Caroline and Liz were quite familiar with each other, meeting over an interview for a job at Jim's restaurant.

A hospitality professional, Caroline had heard that a retired hockey player was opening an eatery in Kelowna, so she went to inquire. The first time she met Jim, his pants were literally falling down. He was playing the part of the plumber, doing whatever was required to get the restaurant up and running. "Go talk to my wife," were the first words Caroline heard him say.

"Liz was beautiful, but not gorgeous in the conventional way. I found her really intimidating at first," Caroline admits. "She just seemed so strong and self-confident. Like, she'd wear her hair short in an era when women didn't. And she was opinionated, but not to the point where she offended people.

"She asked me if I had a cigarette, and a half-hour later she hired me. Then we worked our butts off to get the restaurant open. Some people thought we'd never open on time, but we stayed up really late the night before and sure enough, we did it."

Proud of not only their group effort to succeed, but her considerable involvement in Jim and Liz's conjoined past, Caroline says, "Jim and Liz were role models for me — their love was so strong. They would argue, tell each other to 'F' off, and laugh. I was single, my daughter was two years old, and I'd never seen a relationship like the one they had.

"They just created a great environment for everyone. We'd all sit around after a hard night's work, and the stories would come out. Everything from how Jim's Corvette burst into flames on their honeymoon to how it wasn't easy being a hockey wife.

"Like when husbands weren't permitted to attend their children's birth, because the team always had to come first. Or once, Liz had cooked a special dinner for Jim and he didn't come home on time because he was out drinking with Bobby. Liz had quite the temper, so she left his cold dinner in the driveway. I don't think I could have taken the hockey lifestyle myself.

"It's not that I'm not open to alternative lifestyles. I am. I've lived a few myself and probably will again one day. Even late-night restaurant life can be hard on a couple. But that's not what went wrong with Jim's restaurant. That place was popular, but it needed a liquor licence that it never got, so it didn't work out. But Liz and I kept in contact. She was a real comfort to me when my mom died. Liz had really fine hair, and she'd say, 'One day it's all going to fall out anyway,' and she would laugh. She knew there was a lot of cancer in her family. Then, there she was — 50 years old and dying." Caroline shakes her head in disbelief. "The cancer was in her for seven years. She was getting treatment in Vancouver and no one knew what to do, but there was Liz making everyone feel they were doing so much.

"The only time I remember her getting mad at me was when I made a joke about Jim and she lost patience with me. Jim had been so good to her throughout her sickness. He had lifted her in and out of the bath when she couldn't take care of herself, and she wasn't going to let *me* make fun of him."

With the little finger on her left hand, Caroline pulls gently at her eye when a tiny tear starts to form. "Liz's funeral was so large. She knew everyone. She was a fabulous lady. So Jim and I grieved her loss together. There's a picture of her on our fridge on which she wrote: 'I will always love you.' So now, when I get pissed off at Jim, like when he's being hard-headed or when he's in so much pain he can't help but be a jerk, I'll look at that picture and ask, 'Okay, Liz, help me out here. How did you deal with him when he did what he's doing now?'

"A word that comes to mind for me, David, when I think about what Jim needs to manage his emotions, is *protection*. I feel like Jim needs protection, which is ironic because he played professional hockey, for goodness' sake. He doesn't need protection. But I feel like he needs protection from the things that have harmed him — things like hockey or the people around hockey."

"We started with three rabbits," Jim says when I speak to him and Caroline together. "Mostly for the kids, but Caroline and I like having animals around too."

"Jim's an animal whisperer," Caroline adds.

We are hanging out in their condo's outdoor common area. I push for clarification, and Jim explains how he's always had a way with animals, since he was a child. "Hummingbirds just land in my hand," he says. "I know a guy who managed his animals with a shovel. It got so I couldn't be around him some days."

Caroline: "That guy treated his wife the same way."

Jim nods agreement at Caroline's comment. "I built a little pen for those rabbits. I put it on concrete slabs and we fixed them up a nice run. One of those rabbits was house-trained. It would sleep with the dog and cat. The dog was a big chocolate lab named Gump. He was a 50th birthday present for me from Liz.

"We picked dandelions for those rabbits, gave them carrots, and bought them proper rabbit food. Some we'd let out of the pen now and then.

"It's not that we were surprised when they started to reproduce — we know how fast rabbits work. But while we'd seen them tunnelling under the concrete, I don't think we recognized what was going on under those slabs. And we didn't know everything about rabbits — like how the parents kill the babies sometimes."

Then, despite — or perhaps because of — the dark talk about carnal acts and killing, the couple suddenly smile at each other, sharing a private laugh, I'm sure. "We were having fun. We named the first five or six of them — I think one was called Rocket — and then *boom*! We thought we had 14 maybe. Then we counted them. Turns out we had 23. We thought, 'Oh man, this could be a disaster.'

"The funniest thing was rounding them up. We threw them in the van, I picked up a 20-pound bag of rabbit food, and we took them up into the mountains, to the end of a dead-end road. But one of them wouldn't even get out of the van. They were our pets, for crying out loud. When we started back for the vehicle, they'd follow us.

"For a while, we'd go back to see if they were all right. Sometimes we'd see one or two of them, then we just stopped going, figuring nature would run its course." Jim speaks softly. "You know, maybe some were wild enough to survive; maybe something came along and ate the others.

"My love of nature goes back to when I was a kid. We lived on a small acreage. We had a couple of chickens and I had a pet duck that followed me around. We had pigs to butcher, and one cow. We'd hunt and fish. My brother would grab me and we'd take a can of beans, another of sardines, and a loaf of bread, get on our bikes, and head up the road. He'd cut a little willow and tie on four feet of line, and we'd fish and eat all day.

"Then, in 1972, me, Paul Henderson, [trap-shooting Olympian] Susan Nattrass, and Mike Law [of the Edmonton Eskimos] went to speak at a banquet in the Northwest Territories. That's where I met Merlyn Carter. He was a bush pilot out of Hay River and he had a few fishing camps. Merlyn was later attacked by a bear. His son found him mauled to death.

"Merlyn was a great guy and a great friend. I told him, 'I'd sure like to have a camp up here,' so he sold me one of his. That was the summer I signed with Edmonton. I remember thinking I wanted to play where I could easily get to my hunting camp.

"But my back was hurting so much I couldn't do the work the way I needed to. There were only two cabins, but when you have customers from big American cities, you have to give them a certain kind of service — pulling boats out of the lake, stuff like that. Work I couldn't do anymore.

"So I sold the property back to Merlyn. That was in '86, but for 15 years that camp was one of the highlights of my life. There were caribou there. Sittler helped me build that camp, and Orr helped me put some windows in one of the cabins.

"Another summer I had the whole Hawk team up there. I called it 'Jim Harrison's Northern Outpost.' I had a chance to buy it back after Merlyn died, but I couldn't scrape together the down payment, even if my back had been up for it.

"But I never really let go of that dream. I love the outdoors. Caroline does too. We were running a hockey school in Slave Lake when an RV park came up for sale, so we bought it — a hundred acres on the lake. There were moose, bears . . . we even had a pet fox.

"Caroline and I pulled ourselves out of a hole with that RV park. We sold everything we had. We were selling souvenirs so we could buy that camp. We were just so lucky that the guy selling it was going broke, and he held the mortgage. He said to me, 'If you can get $100,000 together, I'll take it,' because he owed two hundred and eighty grand. Then Caroline and I sold the thing for $550,000. We didn't have any money before that, but all of a sudden we had this opportunity to make two hundred grand. It took us over the hill, because I'd spent all our savings when Liz was sick. It took all my savings to try to save her and make her as comfortable as we could.

"How lucky were Caroline and I that the guy in Slave Lake needed the money? So we sold our house and borrowed off my daughter Ardin to buy that camp. I borrowed off everybody I could. But there was no one to hire to do the work — the oil boom was on. We were paying $40 an hour for a so-called carpenter who couldn't drive a nail.

"Sometimes my back would hurt so much I couldn't get out of bed for two or three days. I was eating Tylenol 3's like they were candy. That RV camp was a good business though. We had it for four years before we had to get rid of it — again, because of my back."

I was curious to see what standard of living Jim and Caroline have today. Because the occasionally convoluted story of Jim's rise and fall from riches rendered me unsure about the situation the Harrisons might be in. I can't be the only person who wondered if any part of Jim's claims for compensation from his former employer, and union, might be a cash grab, that perhaps the Harrisons had lots of money and were simply leveraging legal opportunity.

It turns out Jim and Caroline live pretty typical Canadian lives. They're neither rich nor poor, but they are vulnerable to economic loss. They can't afford to miss many paycheques before they'd be forced to sell something. But in no material way does the Harrison home resemble the Kelowna mansions some of today's hockey players own. Nor is it what you'd expect a businessman who had considerable financial success in the '70s to live in.

"I'm not ashamed of the things that have happened in my life," Jim says. "One time, we were so low on money a friend of mine gave me a job pumping gas at his service station. Some guy pulled in and recognized me, and said, 'Hey, Jim, I didn't know you bought this garage.' I guess I was supposed to be embarrassed to tell him I wasn't the owner, but I didn't care.

"I was making $6.50 an hour when I got talking to one guy and accidently overfilled his tank by 40 bucks. And he wouldn't pay. So they took it off my paycheque. I worked all that week and I had almost no money to show for it. We literally had no money to buy groceries.

"You can put that in the book, I don't care. I had a little Petro-Canada uniform. Here's this famous hockey player pumping gas. You had to do what you had to do. I think I was taking home 180 bucks a week. It wasn't that I didn't enjoy it — it was fun in many ways. But my back couldn't take it, so I had to quit."

Jim drives a full-size pickup truck. There's nothing fancy about it, and it's no longer nearly new. He's got a used motor home that he paid for with inheritance money from his mom. And while he chooses to spend part of his winter in the American South, that's because his kids live there.

"Plus, I get better medical help than I do in Canada," he says unapologetically. "That's the biggest reason I'm asking for assistance from the NHL and the Players' Association; some doctors in Phoenix think they might be able to help me with my back, but I can't afford to pay for the operation."

In recent years, with Caroline's considerable assistance, Jim has weaned himself off painkillers, reduced his alcohol intake, and fit a basic level of exercise and diet into his life. As a result, he has experienced *some* relief.

"I'm obsessive-compulsive; the more my back hurts, the more I eat. The more I eat, the more my back hurts. But the pain has gone away a little in the last few years."

It's been that slight reprieve from pain that has provided Jim with the opportunity to recover from substantial economic loss, because that break from daily discomfort has freed him and Caroline to apply their considerable entrepreneurial spirit toward the buying and selling of their RV park. Jim's talent for finding work hasn't hurt either. "I've taught at hockey schools from Newfoundland to Vancouver Island and as far north as Inuvik," he says. "I've even gone overseas.

"Some of those schools belonged to [former Black Hawks defenceman] Pat Stapleton. Pat's a genius. His focus was skill development long before anyone else's was. He had me touring every town in Newfoundland with guys like Dave Dryden, Marv Edwards, Bill White, Dave Hutchison, and the late Billy Harris. I had my own hockey schools too, in 17 different towns throughout the West and across the Territories."

Understandably proud, it's time for Jim to tell the world what he believes. "I don't care what people think about whether I'm rich or poor," he says. "But I do sort of care what the lawyers think. Those bastards will jump on anything if they think there's a dollar in it. And the Players' Association has so much money that their lawyers can just wait me out. Their only goal is to give me less than what I need to live out the remaining years of my life. I can't promise I have 10 years left, but to the Players' Association and their lawyers, it's just a game.

"If someone wants to take pictures of me picking up a stick in my yard, so be it. I know how my quality of life has been affected. I know how it bothers Caroline that I'm so angry about it. And I haven't forgotten how the whole thing troubled Liz.

"When Brian Burke was vice-president of the NHL, he asked me to send him some documents that showed how the Hawks and Eagleson stole from me. I had to tell Burke that I couldn't afford to pay the courier. So nobody's going to make me feel like I'm some guy who spilled coffee on his lap and then went after the restaurant for a million dollars.

"Do I get a cheque every month from the NHL's emergency

fund? Yes — it supplements my pensions. I'm grateful for that, but it's not enough. And the NHL took that away from me for a while when I needed to cash in some RRSPs. And it's not only the money I'm mad about. It's the principle. There's got to be some human element in what they do. You know, if I was an alcoholic or a drug user, the NHL and the Players' Association would take care of me. But because it's my back, they just want me to go away."

* * * * * * * * * * * * * * * *

Writing this book has been important to me. The interviewing and writing process has helped me to sort through my thoughts. It's helped me to take control of my own sad and angry ideas — let me organize them in ways that make such demons easier to exorcise. Writing set me up to do important emotional work — work that could only occur because my childhood hero gave me countless hours of time on the telephone and an open invitation to his home.

And it's on that phone and in that home that I've come to conclude that Jim Harrison is a bigger hero to me today than he was when I was a child. Not because he played pro hockey, but because of what he accomplished in spite of the game.

Jim wants this book to be something Caroline and his kids can be proud of. "That's right," he says. "I think if we do this right, if we do this properly, if we do this well, I'll be happy.

"I mean, we didn't set our goal at a million dollars or anything. And I feel different about *our* relationship than I did when we started. Sometimes I think I should be a smart man, and you've helped me to be okay with that. I always wanted to be a lawyer. I know I'm talking way over my head now, about our relationship and my hopes and dreams — I'm talking way over my head for a drunken old-time hockey player who didn't finish high school. But I like what you're doing. I think it's going to work out good, unlike some other parts of my hockey life *lately*."

I ask what his emphasis on "lately" is about. "I mean I met with the Players' Association last week. I'm not sure why I didn't tell you. I was going to. I think it's got something to do with something you said when you began our book. Something about how talking about writing is okay, but sometimes it's better to just write and not to talk so much. I think I did something like that last week with the Players' Association. I just decided I should go see them in Toronto.

"I told them I was ready to settle my lawsuit. I reminded them that I'm a victim of Alan Eagleson when *he* ran the Players' Association and how my legal story is well-documented in Russ Conway's book *Game Misconduct*. I told them about how my situation played a role in putting Eagleson in jail and how doing that helped *all* players, past and present.

"I reminded them I suffered a career-ending back injury and that when I did, Eagleson refused to release some important documents, putting me in a position where I was forced to accept a 50 percent buyout of my Black Hawk contract. I showed them how that alone cost me almost 125 grand, in 1978 dollars. I told them how Eagleson prevented me from receiving $175,000 in disability insurance and how he stated incorrectly, and illegally, that I didn't qualify for workers' compensation. I reminded them how I didn't receive proper medical treatment that I was entitled to at the time.

"I told those Players' Association guys that everybody other than them has tried to help me, that had it not been for payments from the NHL emergency fund, former players, and NHL alumni, especially during Liz's fight with cancer, that we would have been unable to make ends meet. I showed them how today I live on my NHL pension of less than 600 bucks a month, CPP disability of $760 a month, NHL emergency fund of $1,000 a month, and whatever work I can come up with. But that my back limits what I can do.

"I told them it was the Supreme Court of British Columbia that said I had to go after them — after the Players' Association — because they're liable for Eagleson's actions. I pointed out how I've always been reasonable under the circumstances, and that that hadn't changed, and that I would be willing to consider a fair offer from them if they were interested in settling — if they were interested in making things right.

"I said I wanted to get on with exploring the possibility of laser surgery with a doctor in Phoenix, but I needed to know if the [Players' Association] could give me any additional support to help pay for such an expensive procedure. I asked, 'If any of this laser surgery left me more crippled, would Caroline and I be looked after in any way?'"

"What'd they say, Jim?" I ask.

A long pause. "They laughed at me."

"They *laughed* at you?"

"They literally laughed at me."

"What are you going to do now?"

"Caroline and I bought some land. We found a piece of property near Greenwood, in the most southern part of B.C., between Grand Forks and Osoyoos. It's called Jewel Lake. It used to be an old mining community; now it's a fishing camp. We've scraped together all the cash we can. We've remortgaged our condo, borrowed from my kids, sold some memorabilia — do you know anyone who wants to buy my leather Leaf jacket?

"It's time to sell all kinds of stuff. Things are falling into place for us — Caroline's son is growing up and soon he'll be going off to college in Kelowna, so he's going to live in our condo and she can go visit him whenever she wants. He's the biggest reason we've stayed in Kelowna as long as we have. I've wanted acreage for a long time — Caroline has too — but we couldn't afford it in Kelowna, and Caroline wasn't willing to leave her son during his high school years. I don't blame her. I wouldn't want someone telling me I had to move away from my kids.

"We're not exactly sure how we're going to manage it, but as long as my back holds out I'm going to give it everything I've got. I need to get busy doing the stuff I love again — like building things and driving tractors. I'm even thinking about buying myself a sawmill. I know that's crazy, but . . .

"We want a dog and a donkey. I want kids around. I want to see the look on the kids' faces when my donkey starts to hee-haw. I want to see their expression when I ask them if they want to go get their parents so they can take that donkey for a walk. I'm hoping old-time hockey fans will bring their kids and their grandkids fishing at our camp.

"I want to buy Caroline an old truck. How about that, eh? Some women want a Mercedes, but Caroline wants an old, beat-up truck. And I want to build her a drive shed to park it in."

Jim's talking tenderly — as loving as I've seen from him. "I went to a track meet the other day, in Tuscon, with my grandson. Lots of 13-year-olds don't want to spend time with their grandfather, so when he asked me to go, I jumped on it. It was wonderful. I told him, 'No computers or cellphones.' He's a great kid — an amazing athlete. He was partially paralyzed when a golf ball hit him in the head, but he still competes in track. Lucky for me there is still a grandchild or two that I can watch grow up.

"But more than anything, I want my relationship with Caroline to keep getting better and stronger. Other than that, we'll see how it goes. It's obvious that the way the Players' Association is — the way they've always been — isn't working for me, and probably never will. I think that's because players are so competitive that even when their playing career is over, some of them have to win at everything they do. It doesn't matter to them who they hurt. They don't understand the idea of looking after one of your own. I think they were quite happy that they won this battle with me, that they don't have to help me with my medical expenses.

"They know that further legal action won't be good for my health, even if I could afford to fight them. That probably pleases them. It's like when we played and you knew a guy on the other team was injured. You'd go after him. You'd zero in on wherever he was hurting — his shoulder, knee, groin . . . it didn't matter. You would hit him every chance you got. I think that's what the Players' Association is trying to do to me. They're only too happy to hit me where I'm hurting.

"It's also clear that the way *I've* been doing things isn't working. I'm spending too much time being angry. About the only thing I know right now is I've got some great kids, super grandkids, and an incredible woman in Caroline. And now we've got a beautiful piece of property. I'm going to try to keep that in mind. Because I realize that *I* need to find a new way to be tough, and I've come to see that Caroline and our kids are the only things really worth fighting for."

* * * * * * * * * * * * * * * * * *

It's the start of the second period — Leafs vs. Flyers, February 6, 1971. Toronto trails by a goal. I'm watching 40 years later.

Any intrigue at the time stemmed from the big deal completed earlier in the week. Not that the hockey played in the first period of this Maple Leaf Gardens game was not enjoyable. Just that there was an interesting backstory to this February affair when the teams swapped goaltenders Bruce Gamble and Bernie Parent, and the Leafs sent the Flyers Mike Walton, who no longer wanted to play in Toronto. Philadelphia then packaged Walton off to Boston for two young forwards including Rick MacLeish, who would figure prominently in the Flyers' future. A couple of draft picks were also exchanged, one of which Toronto would use to select a serviceable scorer in Rick Kehoe.

Leaf captain Davey Keon looks fantastic — seeing so much, and able to translate what he does see into subtle little passes in tight traffic. Harrison is no slouch either. He and his left wing Brian Spencer are banging and crashing while, on Jim's right side, George Armstrong demonstrates the savvy that has served him so well for 20 seasons.

Once again it is Keon vs. Clarke. I notice the Leaf emblem at center ice is only one-tenth the size of insignias found on playing surfaces today, and wonder if bigger is better or if the game can no longer sell itself without tasteless kitsch.

The puck rolls to the boards, and Garry Monahan wastes no time finishing a solid check. Jim Dorey and Billy MacMillan do a beautiful job, between the blue lines, of putting Keon in the clear. Davey dekes Gamble just enough to open his legs and slide the puck between them for his 26th goal of the year. Score tied at one, the period is not yet a minute old.

After watching the previous period on my laptop, I'm now viewing the second on a tiny TV. It's funny how I have far more instant replay in my remote than the network had when the game first aired. I back things up, slow them down, and pause when I want — in such ways that I can better see what has happened than play-by-play broadcaster Bill Hewitt and his colour man Bob Goldham can.

I see that the Henderson/Ullman/Ellis line — or, as a homemade sign in the end seats says, "The HUE line," has no colour. They'll finish the season as three of the team's top four scorers, but they have no jump tonight. Ullman's not his usual crafty self, Henderson is fighting the puck, and Ellis struggles to find the net.

I like the way goalie Plante keeps the puck moving. He's not the only player who chooses an occasional high-risk option — McKenny's not scared either, carrying the puck in front of his own net or deep into the other team's end. Some players actually rag the puck when they're killing a penalty. Coaches must not have been over-studying odds in that era.

No sooner does Goldham provide a prescient comment regarding sophomore Bobby Clarke's promising future than Clarke threads a lovely long pass to the fleet-footed MacLeish. Plante makes a difficult save look easy. It's interesting to compare how much more efficiently Plante plays than Gamble, unlike today's goalies, who I find impossible to tell apart. I wonder why Parent didn't start for the Leafs tonight, and why nobody seems to want to say.

"Ellis ran into Van Impe and was knocked down," Hewitt tells us, before Ullman, Bernier, and MacLeish do what teams in trouble used to do, when players held the puck against the boards with their feet and waited for a whistle. "Ullman, trying to get the puck loose . . ." It doesn't look that way to me. "It's against the boards. Play is called." I've no idea where that tedious play-stopping practice came from, but I'm glad this part of the old game is almost gone.

"Ten thirty-four to go in the second period," and Gamble's got to play great to keep his new team in the game, before Ullman pulls Jim Johnson down from behind. Two minutes for holding. Harrison and Armstrong are called on to kill the penalty.

"Up it comes to André Lacroix, the center, number 7." Lacroix approaches the Leafs' blue line. "He waits," and suddenly, with legitimate hype from Hewitt, "his pass, intercepted by Harrison! He's going in alone! Right in on goal! He's dumped! He scores!" A slight pause from Hewitt, before he explains how "Harrison shot it into the net as he fell!" Jim's short, choppy strides make me smile.

Then, shook up from his collision with Gamble and the goalpost, Jim gets up slowly, and alone. Celebration was minimal compared to today's orgies. It leaves me believing that, in '71, scoring was expected of a man, and that excessive celebration might insult your opponent. Best not to do that, everyone agreed.

Trainer Joe Sgro opens and closes the door to the bench, welcoming the shorthanded hero home. Someone out of sight pats Jim on the back while he takes a seat, but he still seems unsure of his surroundings. "That gives the Leafs the lead for the first time in the game," says Hewitt. "It comes with a minute thirty-three left in Ullman's penalty — Harrison's 11th goal of the year." With Jim dazed, Monahan helps Armstrong complete the penalty kill.

Pelyk rocks Bernier. Then the Leafs, caught with an unusual combination of Keon, MacMillan, and Ullman on, make one too many passes. Another scramble ensues, and all three men again come close. Keon is robbed by Gamble, and then nobody can hit the net. Flyers, feeling pressured, attempt an icing, but Plante, sensing value in keeping the game going, touches the puck and promptly passes to McKenny.

I notice Kitchener's Gary Dornhoefer has not been playing much for the Flyers and that Goldham has just called Jacques Plante "Jack Plant," when Van Impe puts the clutch on Ullman. The referee incorrectly calls Larry Hale for the holding penalty. "I think Larry Hale is probably feeling a little bit of injustice here," Goldham guesses. Either way, Leafs have a man advantage with six minutes left in the second.

The Harrison line, with Dorey and McKenny playing the points, does everything but put the puck in the net. "That hit a goalpost, then a leg. Dorey's got it. Right in on goal!" before the Flyers again ice it. Trying to catch Philadelphia in a change of personnel, Plante skates all the way to the blue line this time. He again passes to McKenny, who, after a nifty move in the Flyers zone, slides the puck over to Monahan at the side of the net, forcing Gamble to make a superb save.

Keon hits a goalpost before passing the puck to the point. Then, just when Larry Hale steps out of the penalty box, Ricky Ley feeds another nice pass to Monahan, who now buries it. Leafs have a two-goal lead. Hewitt: "Monahan from Ley and Keon, and just prior to that, you've seen Gamble coming up with some tremendous acrobatics."

Van Impe cross-checks Ullman. "Philadelphia Flyers pressing now, trailing 3 to 1." MacMillan gets away with a high stick on Clarke, and the second period is over.

Seven minutes and 24 seconds left in the game, Toronto 4, Philadelphia 1, because Harrison has scored again, his second goal of the night, from Spencer.

Dorey attempts a long pass for Ellis, but it's too far. Gamble touches it, so there'll be no icing. He gives it to Hale for Philadelphia. Hale to Simon Nolet. To Bill Lesuk. He scores! A nice shot by Bill Lesuk! It's 4 to 2. Lesuk from Nolet and Hale, with 6:28 left. I'm happy for Bill and his wife Mary Jane who were so good to Jim and others in Oklahoma City.

With 4:29 to go, Plante puts the puck in the corner. Dorey shoots it off the boards for Henderson, who puts it back to McKenny. McKenny's clearing pass goes into the crowd, just missing two women in magnificent fur coats and matching hats.

Three minutes and four seconds left. Clarke's got it. Ullman gets a piece of him. Henderson's dumped, there's no penalty on the play. The puck goes outside the blue line before Nolet brings it back in offside.

Fifty-eight seconds left, Philadelphia tries to get something going. But the Leafs keep them hemmed in, making it difficult for the Flyers to get Gamble out of the net in exchange for an extra attacker.

Thirty-three seconds — Nolet makes a long pass to Lew Morrison. Morrison dumps it in and goes after it. Gamble is out of the net! Here they come. Nolet shoots it in. Plante leaves it for

McKenny. McKenny bangs it off the boards. It's out! A race for it! Henderson gets to it first and scores into the empty Flyer net, but the play is called offside with one second left. No goal.

Game over?

HARRISON, Jim

James David¹ "Max"   C – R. 5'11", 185 lbs.   b. Bonnyville, Alberta, 7/9/1947

REGULAR SEASON

Season	Club	League	GP	G
1963-64	Kamloops Rockets	BCJHL	25	8
1964-65	Estevan Bruins	SJHL	25	2
1965-66	Estevan Bruins	SJHL	60	39
	Estevan Bruins	Mem-Cup	13	10*
	Edmonton Oil Kings	Mem-Cup	6	2
1966-67	Estevan Bruins	CMJHL	47	34
1967-68	Estevan Bruins	WCJHL	46	32
	Estevan Bruins	Mem-Cup	14	19*
1968-69	**Boston Bruins**	**NHL**	**16**	**1**
	Oklahoma City Blazers	**CHL**	**43**	**13**
1969-70	**Boston Bruins**	**NHL**	**23**	**3**
	Toronto Maple Leafs	**NHL**	**31**	**7**
1970-71	**Toronto Maple Leafs**	**NHL**	**78**	**13**
1971-72	**Toronto Maple Leafs**	**NHL**	**66**	**19**
1972-73	Alberta Oilers	WHA	66	39
1973-74	Edmonton Oilers	WHA	47	24
1974-75	Team Canada	Summit-74	3	0
	Cleveland Crusaders	WHA	60	20
1975-76	Cleveland Crusaders	WHA	59	34
1976-77	**Chicago Black Hawks**	**NHL**	**60**	**18**
1977-78	**Chicago Black Hawks**	**NHL**	**26**	**2**
1978-79	**Chicago Black Hawks**	**NHL**	**21**	**4**
	New Brunswick Hawks	AHL	2	0
1979-80	**Edmonton Oilers**	**NHL**	**3**	**0**
	NHL Totals		**324**	**67**
	Other Major League Totals		232	117

WCJHL First All-Star Team (1968). Traded to **Toronto** by **Boston** for Wayne Carleton, Dec. 10, 1969. Selected by **Calgary-Cleveland** (WHA) in 1972 WHA General Player Draft, Feb. 12, 1972. WHA rights traded to **Alberta** (WHA) by **Cleveland** (WHA) for cash, May 1972. Traded to **Cleveland** (WHA) by **Edmonton** (WHA) for Ron Buchanan, Oct. 14, 1974. Rights traded to Chicago by Toronto for Chicago's second-round choice (Bob Gladney) in 1977 Amateur Draft, Sept. 28, 1976. Traded to Edmonton by Chicago for future considerations, Sept. 24, 1979.

| | | | PLAYOFFS | | | | |
A	Pts	PIM	GP	G	A	Pts	PIM
11	19	...	...	...	...	...	...
5	7	40	...	...	...	...	...
37	76	119	11	8	1	9	21
5	15	52*	...	...	...	...	...
3	5	11	...	...	...	...	...
40	74	179	8	2	4	6	38
43	75	222	14	13*	22*	35*	29
15	34*	42	...	...	...	...	...
2	3	21	...	...	...	...	...
13	26	130	9	3	2	5	6
1	4	16	...	...	...	...	...
10	17	36	...	...	...	...	...
20	33	108	6	0	1	1	33
17	36	104	5	1	0	1	10
47	86	93	...	...	...	...	...
45	69	99	...	...	...	...	...
1	1	9	...	...	...	...	...
22	42	106	5	1	2	3	4
38	72	62	3	0	1	1	9
23	41	97	2	0	0	0	0
8	10	31	...	...	...	...	...
5	9	22	...	...	...	...	...
0	0	0	...	...	...	...	...
0	0	0	....	...	...	...	...
86	153	435	13	1	1	2	33
152	269	360	8	1	3	4	13

---

1. Jim's birth certificate actually reads, "Jimmy David."

* lead league

Get the eBook FREE!

At ECW Press, we want you to enjoy this book in whatever format you like, whenever you like. Leave your print book at home and take the eBook to go! Purchase the print edition and receive the eBook free. Just send an email to ebook@ecwpress.com and include:

- the book title
- the name of the store where you purchased it
- your receipt number
- your preference of file type: PDF or ePub?

A real person will respond to your email with your eBook attached. Thank you for supporting an independently owned Canadian publisher with your purchase!